HEALING WOMEN'S EMOTIONS

HEALING WOMEN'S EMOTIONS

by
Paula Sandford

Victory House, Inc.
Tulsa, Oklahoma

Unless otherwise noted, all Scripture is taken from the *New American Standard Bible* © 1960, 1963, 1968, 1971, 1972, 1973, 1975, 1977, by the Lockman Foundation. Used by permission.

Dedication

This book is lovingly dedicated to my husband,
John

Foreword

I have attempted to write concerning subjects about which I am most often asked questions. I don't pretend to have all the answers, but I assure you that those which I offer have been tried, tested and lived in a practical way over a great many years. I believe they will be helpful to those who make them their own.

I have not addressed the issue of sexual abuse, though I see it as the most emotionally damaging experience a woman can endure, because I have already written seven chapters on this very important subject in my book, *Healing Victims of Sexual Abuse,* published by Victory House, Inc. in 1988. A great number of abuse victims have told me that it has brought them more healing than any other book they have read on the subject, and many counselors have also expressed their appreciation and recommended it to their clients.

I pray that *Healing Women's Emotions* will become a blessing of insights and understandings for all women. May those understandings become tools to better enable them to handle their emotions in redemptive and constructive ways.

I also hope that men who read this book will be enlightened concerning the women with whom they live and work. And I earnestly pray that they might become better equipped to respect, cherish, nurture and protect the mysterious gifts God has given to them —

womanly gifts which will rarely fit the size and shape
of man-made boxes.

— Paula Sandford

Contents

Contents

1
Happy to Be Me

I enjoy being a woman.

Even though I have sometimes felt frustrated or angry when confronted by double standards and ignorant, biased opinions concerning the place and value of women in our society, I have never seriously entertained jealousies of men or dreams of relinquishing who I am for any other identity. The realities of greater advantage in areas of job opportunity, recognition and reward available to the male of the species (just because he is male), have never seemed to be so appealing to me that I would, if I could, exchange places with a man.

Nor would I exchange my experiences as daughter, sister, wife, mother, grandmother, or great-grandmother. Though I must admit that sometimes I don't *like* me, I have come to like *being* me. And more importantly, I have learned to *love* me, as God himself does.

Life brings endless varieties of trials, struggles, disappointments, wounds, victories and blessings. I have known and struggled with powerful emotions in response to all of these. Like most other people, I have spent time wallowing in feelings, stewing in self-righteousness and anger, making up speeches. I have struggled with self-condemnation for failing to live up

1

to expectations I put upon myself. Some of my feelings have rolled verbally eloquent from an unruly tongue — and some have nearly blown a fuse inside of me.

Over the years, by the grace and loving discipline of the Lord, I have been taught redemptive ways of handling these inner fires. I have come to know and appreciate that the distinctly female sensitivities which allow me to feel emotionally devastated or driven are the *same* ones that enable me to experience the blessing to soar and sing with every part of my being. Or to carry others in my heart as really as I would carry a child within my womb, travailing until Christ be formed in them (Gal. 4:19).

The difference lies in what I am able to *do* with my feelings, and that is the subject of this book.

The cultural limitations put upon women will continue to change because that is part of mankind's sin and God's redemptive plan. Some of those changes may happen only as women step forward to speak out for equal opportunity and justice. But the ability of an individual to experience and participate freely in fullness of life before, as, and after *exterior* bondages and barriers have been broken, depends upon the condition of one's own heart. If the Lord is allowed to minister to the depths of us, we will be healed *interiorly* and set free to become all that we can be — in our homes, in the Church, in the marketplace, and in the world.

We will know our identity and our worth regardless of the circumstances in which we live or the yet-unchanged attitudes and actions of the people with whom we are in relationship. We will be free to make decisions concerning difficult situations and oppressive relationships according to the calling and direction of the Lord. We will not be in bondage to legalisms or compulsive needs to succeed, or please, or belong, or to be the savior and redeemer of another person's life.

I am who I am as a gift of God. I sometimes cringe when some well-meaning individual tries to elevate and honor me by neutering me. I do not aspire to be a "chair-*person*" I am honored to be a "chair-*woman*," and will attempt to be myself in any such position, with dignity, authority, common sense, skill and sensitivity to others that is enhanced by my sexuality, not hampered by it.

I grieve for some who fight so energetically and angrily for male privilege and recognition that they unconsciously destroy their own qualities of femininity and forfeit the greater portion of their birthright. On the other hand, I grieve even more for the woman who thinks so little of herself that she lays her glory down like a doormat in the delusion of false submission, and invites a man to wipe his feet on her.

Recently a Christian psychiatrist friend gave me a copy of a very interesting and enlightening article from one of his professional journals. One statement in the article, if heeded, might threaten to turn someone's chauvinist world upside-down.

The notion of male superiority is neither a case of anatomy as destiny nor is it a psychological truism. In fact, clinical evidence demonstrates the opposite to be true, that females enjoy not only biological superiority, but psychological superiority.

(*Psychiatric Annals* 15: 12 December 1985, "The Myth of Male Superiority: Its Biopsychosocial Importance to Male Psychological Development," Dr. Paul F. Giannandrea, MD, p. 722)

I rather enjoyed reading that statement, and was very much enlightened by the data which explained it. However, I didn't need it to make me feel good about myself.

If the attitude of others toward me as a woman makes the performance of my office or expression of my identity or calling more difficult, I will still know who I am, and receive their resistance as another exercise in forgiveness. Sometimes as my husband and I have gone out to teach, the opening session has been much more difficult for me than for him. I have keenly felt walls of resistance, "What can she, a woman, have to say to me?" Those barriers were melted down each time before our teaching was half finished, but before the breakthrough, I had to spend energy to rise above the blockage.

Many times pastors and others have graciously and humbly confessed and asked my forgiveness for having brought that sort of blocking prejudice into a meeting. Such confessions may tempt me to nurse my feelings of, "Not fair! Why should my sex be an issue? We were both invited here, but John is free to concentrate fully on teaching because he doesn't have to fight such ridiculous resistance!" On the other hand, such an opportunity may lead me to choose gratitude for a victory won.

If I were not basically secure in who I am despite what anyone thinks of me, that choice would be very difficult. Especially if no one did apologize. But insofar as I am secure, I can meet and accept others where they are with no personal threat to my self-esteem, and no compulsive need for self-defense.

Occasionally, however, I meet an individual who repeatedly refers to one of the books my husband and I have co-authored as "John's book." In such a case I may call it to their attention that *we* wrote the book together.

Almost invariably such a person will respond with a question, "How do you do that?" This gives me the opportunity to share something this generation needs to hear again and again — husbands and wives *can* work together successfully, even when sensitive issues are involved. This has been illustrated many hundreds of times as we have submitted our written material to one another to invite appreciated criticism and correction, and as we have trusted God with what comes out of the other's mouth as we have taught together.

My husband and I have been married for forty-one years as I write these words. He loves to tell people that marriage is a 24-hour-a-day exercise in forgiveness. We can laugh at that together now. In the early years of our marriage our experience of "getting to know you" was often a mixture of pain and ecstasy. Now, six children, fifteen grandchildren, and two great grandchildren later, I can testify to the very practical truth of Romans 5:1-5:

> Therefore having been justified by faith, we have peace with God through our Lord Jesus Christ, through whom also we have obtained our introduction by faith into this grace in which we stand; and we exult in hope of the glory of God. And not only this, but we also exult in our tribulations, knowing that tribulation brings about perseverance; and perseverance, proven character; and proven character, hope; *and hope does not disappoint, because the love of God has been poured out within our hearts* through the Holy Spirit who was given to us.

Married or single, how do you take hold of hope and peace and love and glory in the midst of an increasingly sinful generation? For those whose lifelong struggle has been to live with alcoholics or abusive behavior, "we exult in our tribulations" doesn't sound like anything but masochistic craziness. For those who desperately want to love and nurture loved ones who consistently shut them out, "hope does not disappoint" seems like an empty promise.

Continually reinforced feelings of rejection can drag us down into a realm of futility. Making sense of such things, and learning to live healthily with our emotions before we see any evidence of redemption in people or any change of circumstances, is what this book is about. And beyond that, healing, which means vastly more than just feeling better.

2
Women's Liberation in the Bible

The question of proper and acceptable roles for men and women has too long been filled with confusion, threat and hurt, emotional striving, attack and defense. In this day when God is moving upon His Church to "restore all things" (Matt. 17:11, Mark 9:12), we especially need to have a sturdy biblical leg to stand on so we can step forward to take hold of the life and good works God has prepared beforehand for us to walk in (Eph. 2:10). This is especially important as we work out our basic relationships. Let's go back to the beginning:

God's Perfect Plan

> And the Lord God said, 'It is not good that the man should be alone; I will make him an helpmeet for him.' (Gen. 2:18, KJV)

It is important to note here that the word "helpmeet" means "a power equal to man." *Equal* power does not necessarily mean *same* power. Some versions of the Bible use the word "helper." But let us understand that the female "helper" that God provides for man from his rib (the area of his heart) is intended to be a helpmeet, one who is designed to *meet* her husband.

She is not just an incidental, though helpful appendage, and certainly not inferior in quality or value.

It was not good for man to be alone. It is ridiculous to think that God created man and afterwards found that he had forgotten something which necessitated a little addendum. Woman is in no way a postscript. God knew *from the beginning* that it was not good for man to be alone. And so He created woman with the pre-planned intent that she and the man would complement, bless, nurture and upbuild one another. His plan for their duality was His best hope and device for the fullness of their maturation, so that He might have fellowship with His growing children.

> And the man said, 'This is now bone of my bones, and flesh of my flesh; she shall be called Woman, because she was taken out of Man.' For this cause a man shall leave his father and mother, and shall cleave to his wife; and they shall become one flesh."
> (Gen. 2:23,24)

Man and woman were designed by God from the beginning to be distinctly individual, free to make choices, yet created to be vitally one with each other.

> He created *them* male and female, and He blessed *them,* and named *them Man* in the day when they were created.   (Gen. 5:2)

Each person, male *or* female, was created in the image of God, male *and* female, with both male and female attributes. I have no problem whatsoever calling God "Father" and relating to Him as such. My childhood experiences with my earthly father built into me positive attitudes and comfortable feelings toward men. "Father" to me means a special quality of strength, power, protection, logic and authority. I also knew a tenderness and gentleness flowing from the heart of my father.

Because of that good foundation built in me, I can easily see those qualities flowing in perfection from the heart of my heavenly Father. What we have experienced or judged our fathers to be always colors to some extent our pictures of God, the GREAT authority figure. If I had been neglected or abused by my father, and had with futility longed for him to be what I needed him to be — or if I had learned to identify mother as *the only* one who could understand and comfort — I would probably be among the ranks of those today who lobby for inclusive language in the Bible (using generic pronouns, instead of masculine ones, for deity).

Man is designed to experience and act primarily out of the masculine pole of his being, and yearn for the woman to meet him. In their one-fleshness she will express that part of him which he cannot. Woman is designed to experience and act primarily from a uniquely feminine base, though she has masculine qualities within her. Her husband is to unite with her in such a way as to fulfill and express easily that masculine part of her which she cannot.

My parents, imperfect as they were, represented to me an unusually healthy balance of gentle, strong, *masculine* father *united* with a tender, strong, *feminine* mother. He was the head of the house, though profoundly influenced by her. When he was gone from home as a traveling salesman, she managed very capably under varieties of stress; and he was a powerful balm to settle her emotions the moment he came through the door.

I called him father, but never thought of him apart from mother. They were a unit. For that reason I have no difficulty understanding how God could create man and woman and call *them* Man. When the Bible says: "he" — "him" — "his," I know that means me and mine as well. And when I call God "Father," I never think of Him apart from gentleness and tenderness.

There Is Healing for Those Whose Father-Image Was Negative or Fractured.

For those who were terribly wounded by fathers (or other authority figures), and now find blockages in relation to Father God, the beginning of freedom is to choose to forgive your earthly father. Forgiveness does not excuse his transgressions or his abdication of authority and affectionate nurture. He will stand accountable before God.

On the other hand, forgiveness of another person has little to do with the actual guilt of those who are being forgiven. The supposed offender may be innocent. Or he may be guilty of even more than the wounded party is aware. To choose to forgive is to say, "I am angry. I have held resentment and bitterness in my heart against my father (or whoever it is). I recognize that this is poison inside of me. It will prevent or destroy life in me and others. It colors my perceptions and can pollute every relationship I try to develop. I want to be rid of it so that I may bless others and be free to trust God."

When a choice to forgive is made, in prayer, the Lord takes that choice and makes it real. It may be necessary to repeat the choice again and again. After all, powerful resentments were built by a series of choices in reaction to pain that may have spanned years. We may even be afraid to let anger or resentment go, because it has seemed to be our only defense. Without it, we fear being overcome by those who would violate us.

If we have already tried again and again in our own strength to forgive, and now come to prayer with the realization that we are helpless to accomplish it alone, we may experience a miracle of release — because our heart is ripe. The Lord will let us struggle as much as necessary in the process of choosing in order to write the necessity of our intention and other lessons indelibly upon our hearts. But He will be faithful to accomplish this goal, because it is His will to heal and set free.

When the poison of unforgiveness is finally gone from our hearts, we are then able to receive the fullness and comfort of healing and affirmation from Father God. We will have eyes to see and ears to hear. And the kindness of His healing will then lead us to the blessing of repentance for our own sinful reactions. When we have known the love and kindness of God, we no longer fear acknowledging and taking respon-sibility for our own sin. And we no longer fear vulnerability in relationships. God will build something gloriously new and beautiful on the foundation of forgiveness and repentance.

Man and Woman Complete One Another

In one sense my husband is that other part of me without which I am not *complete*. And I am that part of him. "One flesh" refers to far more than physical union. It is a meeting and uniting of two people in body, mind and spirit.

God's plan for our coming together is *not* ½ + ½ = *one whole*.

The formula for our union is more accurately described as 1 + 1 = one greater and deeper and richer than either of us could be alone, more like the impossible math of 1 x 1 = 100.

For those who understand concepts more clearly when they are pictured, I invite you to see God's plan for husband-and-wife relationships in this diagram:

NOT THIS...............................BUT THIS

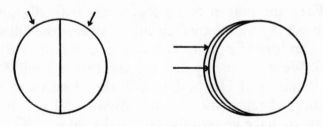

Wholeness Depends Upon the Lord

It is very important to understand that though we are to complete one another in the one-flesh relationship of marriage, a man or woman who never marries is not thereby prevented from becoming whole. Every person's *wholeness* depends upon a developed personal relationship with the Lord Jesus Christ. He is our righteousness and our balance; He gives us our identity and enables us to experience unity.

> For all of you who were baptized into Christ have clothed yourselves with Christ. There is neither Jew nor Greek, there is neither male for female; for you are all one in Christ Jesus.(Gal. 3:27,28)

Ideally our corporate wholeness is to be blessedly completed when all that we are is given into the one-flesh marriage relationship that God has designed. Unfortunately, since sin entered the picture early in the history of mankind, all of us contribute significantly less than individual wholeness to the union.

But the Lord's plan is not defeated. He is able to use our deepest fractures and roughest exteriors powerfully and effectively in His redemptive process when we invite Him to do so. We are blessedly designed to be like abrasives to each other until the Lord in us has accomplished His plan — the polishing of a corporate jewel.

The Beginning of the Battle

The age-old "battle of the sexes" began when *both* woman and man sinned and lied to God about it.

WOMAN

1. Talked to the serpent.
2. Failing in discernment, believed the serpent, and ate of the forbidden fruit, desiring to be like God. (He would have matured her and taught her in His wisdom and timing. She took her life into her own hands.)
3. Seduced her husband to eat with her.

MAN

1. Failed to protect Eve.
2. Failed to communicate clearly which tree was for eating and which was not (Eve was not yet made when the commandments were given).
3. Chose to follow his wife rather than the commandments of God. (This is idolatry.)

If *either* of them had been eating adequately of the Tree of Life in the middle of the Garden (the Lord Jesus), they would not have been so vulnerable to sin. They would not have failed.

The Merciful Love of God, Rejected

Neither took responsibility for her/his own transgression, though God gave each of them ample opportunity to do so. The third chapter of Genesis relates the grandest case of buck-passing in all of history:

And they heard the sound of the LORD walking in the garden in the cool of the day, and the man and his wife hid themselves from the presence of the Lord God among the trees of the garden.

Then the LORD God called to the man, and said to him, *'Where are you?'*

And he said, 'I heard the sound of Thee in the garden, and *I was afraid because I was naked; so I hid myself.'*   (Gen. 3:8-10)

The Lord knew exactly where Adam was, and why. His question gave Adam an opportunity to confess, but he lied. The guilty couple had always known they were naked (Gen. 2:25). They were now ashamed and afraid because they had sinned. They had become defiled by Satan, and were perceiving everything through his eyes. Therefore they could no longer trust the nature of God.

And He said, *'Who told you that you were naked? Have you eaten of the tree of which I commanded you not to eat?'*

And the man said, 'The *woman* whom *Thou* gavest to be with me, *she* gave me from the tree and I ate.'

Then the LORD God said to the woman, *'What is this you have done?'*

And the woman said, 'The *serpent* deceived me, and I ate.'   (Gen. 3:11-13)

Reaping for Sin

Because of sin for which neither of them was repentant, they lost their relationship with God, and the quality of life with which God had originally blessed them. Eve's desire had always been for her husband, now it would be an inordinate desire. She would look for and demand from her husband what only God can give, because of her fractured trust in God and an unholy fear of Him. The pain of bringing forth children would be greatly multiplied (Gen. 2:16). She could no longer rest in God, and stress would always multiply pain.

Adam had always ruled over his wife, but now because of sin, his rule would be possessive, dominating and controlling. Still today there are many religious men who, in their fear, confusion, and unhealed childhood wounds, make a perverted use of the Bible to excuse and perpetuate domination and control over women. The turning point of nearly every movement which has gone into heresy and cultism has been marked by legalism and the subjugation of women.

Marriages have collapsed when husbands have tried to force their wives to be what they wanted, rather than meeting and loving and nurturing them to freely become what God wanted. Husbands were disappointed and disillusioned with what they had "made" because the wives were no longer the adequate counterfoils and helpmeets God had given them; and they didn't have the discernment to see what had gone wrong. Many women, eager to please, but insecure about their own identities and worth, have allowed and even invited men to treat them so.

The relationship of man and woman with the earth would necessarily be characterized by toil and sweat.

And the whole "creation was subjected to futility" (Rom. 8:20). God *had* to turn the power down because of the sinfulness of Man (man and woman, Gen. 5:2). They would have destroyed the creation and themselves.

Good News

Now for the good news! God does not intend to leave us that way! He has, in Jesus Christ, already begun to restore us to the glory we had in the beginning! Hear this:

> *For I consider that the sufferings of this present time are not worthy to be compared with the glory that is to be revealed to us.* For the anxious longing of the creation waits eagerly for the revealing of the sons of God. For the creation was subjected to futility, not of its own will, but because of Him who subjected it, in hope that *the creation itself also will be set free from its slavery to corruption into the freedom of the glory of the children of God.* For we know that the whole creation groans and suffers the pains of childbirth together until now. And not only this, but also we ourselves, having the first fruits of the Spirit, even we ourselves groan within ourselves, waiting eagerly for our adoption as sons, the redemption of our body. *For in hope we have been saved,* but hope that is seen is not hope; for why does one also hope for what he sees? But if we hope for what we do not see, *with perseverance we wait eagerly for it.* And in the same way the Spirit also helps our weakness; for we do not know how

to pray as we should, but *the Spirit Himself intercedes for us with groanings too deep for words;* and He who searches the hearts knows what the mind of the Spirit is, because *He intercedes for the saints according to the will of God. And we know that God causes all things to work together for good to those who love God, to those who are called according to His purpose.*(Rom. 8:18-28)

God's Old Testament Purpose and Model for Women
(Proverbs 31:11 ff)

She is valued and called to be all she can be.

We read in Proverbs 31 that an excellent wife is worth far more than jewels. Her husband's heart trusts in her, and he will have no lack of gain. She does him good all the days of her life.

She is industrious, healthy, strong in body, self-confident, ministering to others, and well-dressed.

She affirms her husband and because of that, he has prestige.

She works in the business-world, is unafraid, well-ordered, consistent, and conducts herself with dignity and kindness.

She is not an extension of her husband.

She is rewarded, blessed by her husband and children. The Scripture says,

Her children rise up and bless her; her husband also, and he praises her. . . *Give her the product of*

her hands, and let her works praise her in the gates.
(Prov. 31:28,31).

YAVO Digest recently carried an article by Rachel D. Levine, who is writing her doctoral thesis on women's role in Judaism during the early centuries. She wrote that the Proverbs 31 passage has been held up for hundreds of years as the ideal to which Jewish women should aspire.

What did the woman do, and what were her responsibilities? Within the home, she had total authority to see that all domestic duties were performed, and in addition to her own labors, supervised the work of the servants. She made sure that ample supplies of both food and clothing were available for all household members. What was not locally attainable she imported from other areas if necessary. In addition to providing for her dependents, she was in charge of the 'cottage industry' of her home and dealt with the local merchants in selling them the goods thus produced. She was active in real estate ventures, and supervised the agricultural workers. She ensured the family's survival during hard times by a savings program, and was the prime educator of her children.

In addition to her domestic and commercial ventures, she was active in local charity work. Her religious duties were not neglected, and she was known for her piety and devotion to the Lord. As a result, her husband was free to concentrate on his endeavors without worrying about his household affairs, secure in the knowledge that all was being done properly without the need for his constant supervision.

(Rachel Levine, "The Biblical Woman." *YAVO Digest* Vol 3, No. 6, p. 12. Used by permission. Copyright protected.)

What a contrast this is to the attitude of some men in the modern day who mistakenly have thought that the Bible gives them the mandate and/or license to tell their wives what to wear, cook, think, say, and where to go, what to do, and how to do it!

When one partner so dominates the other, he cancels out the other part of his own flesh. My husband, John, tells people that if I should ever shut my mouth, he would lose half his wisdom. Then he hastens to add with an affectionate chuckle, "But I don't think there is a chance of that ever happening!"

In the Old and New Testaments the woman is called to
give all she can be, and to shine.

No one, after lighting a lamp, puts it away in a cellar, nor under a peck-measure, but on the lampstand, in order that those who enter may see the light. (Luke 11:33)

An excellent wife is the *crown* of her husband.(Prov. 12:4)

In biblical culture, the head is the place of honor. Feet are considered to be the lowest, least-honored part of the body. If the Bible meant for us to dishonor or diminish woman, or give anyone license to walk on her, she would have been called "an old shoe," not a "crown!"

The Bible sets forth the ideal, and much of the Law is written to protect the woman from violation. However, the sin nature being what it is, women have been oppressed in many cultures throughout history. Still, wherever Jesus Christ has not been made Lord of men's hearts, subjugation and persecution of women persists.

God's Original Plan for Male/Female Relationships Is to Be Restored in Christ

Jesus Christ came to bring recovery of sight to the blind, good news to the afflicted, to bind up the brokenhearted, to proclaim liberty to captives, freedom to prisoners, and to set free those who are downtrodden (Isa. 61:1-3 and Luke 4:18). Jesus befriended women, received ministry from them, defended, honored and respected them. He set an example for all to follow.

Saint Paul has unfairly received some bad press from many who in their ignorance of the culture of biblical times are sincerely mistaken. In actuality, he followed Jesus as one of the greatest liberationists of all time. He took care to acknowledge with gratitude those women who had helped significantly in the work of the church: Prisca, Claudia, Phoebe, Mary, Tryphaena, Tryphosa, Rufus' mother, Julia, Nereus' sister, Apphia, and others. In Philippians 4:3 he writes, "Indeed, true comrade, I ask you also to help these women who have shared my struggle in the cause of the gospel."

Let us take a closer look at some often quoted and frequently misunderstood passages from Paul's letters.

Paul Taught Mutual Submission Coupled With Sacrificial Love and Respect.

And be subject to one another in the fear of Christ. Wives be subject to your own husbands **as** to the LORD. For the husband is head of the wife **as** Christ also is head of the church, He Himself being Savior of the body. But **as** the church is subject to Christ, so also the wives ought to be to their husbands in everything.   (Eph. 5:21-24)

Notice first that "be subject to one another" is said in the context of marital relationships. No one had ever before told a man to be subject to a woman, yet here Saint Paul clearly says to be subject to *one another!* Notice that he carefully says first to be subject to one another before going on to describe the husband's position as head of the wife.

Therefore, the following picture is definitely *not* what our Lord or Paul had in mind!

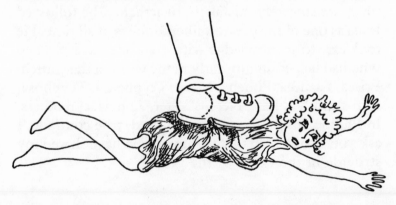

Notice the word "as" which I have put in bold-face type in the Scripture quotes. Paul is presenting a clear model for headship and submission. *How* is Christ head of the Church? By laying down His life for her sake, that she might have life. And by inviting her to accept that gift — never robbing her of her free will. Never forcing her. Never condemning. Never shutting her out. Loving her unconditionally. Strengthening her so she can stand. Protecting her.

How is the Church subject to Christ? By voluntarily offering all that she is, with commitment to love unconditionally, and to serve with sensitivity, faithfulness, honor and respect.

Husbands, love your wives, just **as** Christ also loved the church and **gave Himself up for her;** that He might sanctify her,. . .Husbands ought also to love their own wives **as** their own bodies. He who loves his own wife loves himself, for no one ever hated his own flesh, but *nourishes and cherishes* it, just as Christ also does the church, because we are members of His body.

(Eph.5:25,26,28)

We read here a clear call to *give,* not to *get.* The command is to minister to the other for the other's sake, not self-centeredly demanding from the other, especially not a husband demanding and controlling because of his so-called superior position. Notice the emphasis on the one-flesh nature of husband and wife and the relationship between loving, nurturing, and cherishing.

Love is not merely a romantic feeling. It is a *choice* to nurture and cherish unconditionally so that the spouse might grow in sanctification into the most he/she can be.

It is at the times when I least deserve my husband's cherishing that I most need his love, and certainly his nurture. More than once I have said to John, "I'm upset. I'm a mess. I don't want or need your analysis, your advice, or your rebuke right now. I just need you to hug me!" And when he puts his bewilderment aside to wrap those strong arms around his undeserving wife, I am strengthened to receive all the other things he'd like to present to me. He needs that same consideration from me.

"Let the wife **see to it** that she respect her husband"   (Eph. 5:33).

It is difficult for many women to respect their husbands because they can easily make long lists of their transgressions and failings. But respect is something much more than approval of performance. I am called to "see to it" that I respect my husband's position — not to mother, lacerate, or emasculate him.

I am called to respect him as a person, not only for his admirable qualities, but as one who has problems, feelings, and sensitivities that need to be met according to the nature of Christ in me. It is to our benefit if I respect the fact that his experiences and approach to many situations are often different than mind, and that I am not always comprehensive or right in my perceptions and understandings.

To respect another is not the same as to agree with him. Respect does not prevent appropriate confrontation. Rather, respect calls us to discipline our hearts to maintain attitudes which will affirm the other in every way possible. And to discipline our actions and words to edify, not to undermine or annihilate the other.

Paul emphasized the importance of CORPORATENESS in Christian faith and life, and gave directions for growing in it.

- **Lay aside the old self.**

- **Be renewed in the spirit of your mind.**

- **Put on the new self.**

- **Lay aside falsehood.**

- **Be angry but sin not.**

- **Do not give the devil an opportunity.**

- **Let no unwholesome word proceed from your mouth.**

- **Let bitterness and wrath and anger and clamor and slander be put away from you, and all malice.**

- **Be kind to one another, tender-hearted, FORGIVING EACH OTHER, just as God in Christ also has forgiven you**

(See Eph. 5:15-32)

Clearing Up Misconceptions About Paul's Instructions

Let a woman quietly receive instructions with entire submissiveness. But I do not allow a woman to teach or exercise authority [*USURP authority in KJV*] over a man, but to remain quiet.

Years ago John and I were invited to speak for an ecumenical gathering at a restaurant in St. Louis. The meeting proceeded quietly and smoothly until I stepped to the microphone. A red-faced, portly man instantly jumped to his feet and loudly challenged my right to teach. Quickly, Paul Haglin (the pastor in charge of the meeting), along with my husband, stepped in front of me, and Paul declared with gentle but firm authority that since he had invited me to speak, there was no way in which I could possibly be usurping authority.

The man refused to hear, and his voice rose as he raged on. John said, "It is clear this man has no intention to hear, and intends only to disrupt. Get him out of here." Several men from the host church physically picked him up and carried him outside.

I continued to teach, overwhelmingly grateful that I had been defended by strong, masculine partners in the gospel. I realized also that the experience had brought healing to a place deep inside of me that had still felt unprotected because my father had traveled away from home so much when I was a child. I had prayed about it. This experience confirmed my prayer, and strengthened my faith that my heavenly Father is ever present and ready to take the initiative on my behalf.

Later we learned that this was not that man's first time to be forcefully transported to outer courts; he had usurped authority many times in many places as he set himself up as a self-appointed prophetic "authority" on the Word. He finally "authoritated" his way into a psychiatric ward.

Scripture needs to be read in the context in which it was written.

First Timothy 2:11 was written in the context of the usurping of authority. Also, Paul was well aware that Christians were already upsetting the world (Acts 17:6). He had the wisdom to make it known that he was neither teaching nor modeling extremes which would suddenly and unnecessarily upset established order in the churches. People then, as now, did not accept change with gracious ease.

As a case in point, John and I served in a church in Illinois early in our ministry. Someone gave the church a beautiful new altar. Our logic said that the old altar had served well for an untold number of years. Though it bore the scars of much use, it could serve in another capacity for a long time as well. But the new altar was much more appropriate to the decor of a newly redecorated chancel.

With respect and honor, we moved the old altar to the first floor where the young people could appreciate it in their chapel area, and installed the new one in the main sanctuary. Immediately dissensions crescendoed into accusations and insults! One would have thought that we had moved God!

Paul had also a practical purpose in mind when he said that women should be quiet. First Corinthians 14:26 ff. sets out a reasonable order for considerate participation and sharing in the churches, spelling it out clearly to everyone concerning when it is appropriate for one to speak and another to keep silent.

And the spirits of prophets are subject to prophets for *God is not a God of confusion but of peace,* as in all the churches of the saints.   (1 Cor. 14:32)

The following passage, then, needs to be read in the context of the rest of the chapter, within Paul's concern to preserve order:

Let the women keep silent in the churches; for they are not permitted to speak, but let them subject themselves, just as the Law also says. And if they desire to learn anything, let them ask their own husbands at home; for it is improper for a woman to speak in church.

Was it from you that the word of God *first* went forth? Or has it come to you *only?*

If anyone thinks he is a prophet or spiritual, let him recognize that the things which I write to you are the Lord's commandment.(1 Cor. 14:34-37)

There is certainly no sexist language here:

"Until *we all* attain to the unity of the faith, and of the knowledge of the Son of God, to a mature man, to the measure of the stature which belongs to the fullness of Christ"   (Eph. 4:13).

". . . speaking the truth in love, *we* are to grow up in all aspects into Him, who is the head, even Christ."
(Eph. 4:15)

To understand what is going on here, we need to divest our minds of the pictures we have of our own home groups, with everyone, male and female, seated together in comfortable circles in someone's living room. The Scripture must be read in the context of the culture of the East (that culture remains the same in many aspects throughout the Middle and Far-East). Traditionally men and women were not seated together in the temple worship. Men gathered in the main room; women were seated behind a partition. When people met in homes, even for social gatherings, the men and women were normally separated.

In the late 1950s John and I were privileged to have a beautiful couple, Russell and Vickie Chandran, from India, visit in our home on several occasions. They were Christians doing graduate study for a year at Chicago Theological Seminary, which was then a part of the University of Chicago. He was the president of a theological seminary in Bangalore, and she was a school-teacher. We very much enjoyed our fellowship with them.

As the time approached for them to return to their homeland, Vickie said that she would have to be very careful at home for a time. She had grown accustomed in America to visiting and sharing openly in mixed company. It had been a delight to her, and had become comfortably a part of her.

She was afraid that when she returned home she might forget that such an interchange was not allowed. She might offend someone, thereby disgracing her husband. They were bound by their culture to act in ways neither still believed to be appropriate. We had witnessed the deep love and respect Russell had for his wife. In Christ, he valued her person and her opinion, and welcomed her expression of who she was.

Can you put yourself in the position of a woman in the early church? For centuries there had been much oppression of women everywhere in the eastern world. Despite the ideal set forth in Judaism and described in Proverbs 31, there were still many restrictions upon women, particularly in the area of speaking to or participating with men in public, and in the areas of religious service. A woman could be divorced by her husband if he simply set her belongings on the doorstep. She and her whole family would be disgraced.

That is the principal reason for the New Testament teachings concerning divorce — protection of women — that they not be put out as if they were chattel! Jesus had talked with women, respected, defended and honored them. He came offering a new quality of life to everyone, far beyond their wildest dreams. They had witnessed or heard of miracles that boggled their minds. Today we are so familiar with the teachings of Jesus, and take for granted the freedoms which Christianity has won for us, that we may miss the excitement that was enjoyed in the early Church. Early Christians were on fire! So on fire, in fact, that they were willing to risk their lives.

Christian women had such an excitement building in them they could hardly contain themselves! Imagine yourself in an early church meeting. Earth-shaking things are being talked about in the main room; life-saving matters the Lord has intended for you also. You desperately don't want to miss a word, but you can't hear clearly all that is being said because you are set off to the side with the other women behind some sort of partition (usually a cloth curtain or tapestry). You miss something, and before you can stop to think, you are trying get your neighbor's attention to find out what it was. Perhaps you are whispering across the curtain to your husband, if he is close by, "Ben, what did he say?!" And by so doing, you cause a disturbance.

It is no wonder Paul told the women that if they desired to learn something, they should ask their husbands at home. Paul goes on (in verse 36) to properly reprimand the women for their lack of propriety. "Has it [the Word of God] come to you only?" Their undisciplined excitement had caused them to be self-centeredly inconsiderate of others. But this directive is only part of a chapter which is an appeal for orderliness, self-discipline and consideration of everyone, one for the other, that the whole body might be edified. "Let all things be done properly and in orderly manner"   (1 Cor. 14:40).

Women, according to Scripture, were not excluded from prophesying.

Now this man [Philip the evangelist] had four virgin daughters who were prophetesses. (Acts 21:9)

And there was a prophetess, Anna the daughter of Phanuel, of the tribe of Asher. She was advanced in years, having lived with a husband seven years after her marriage, and then as a widow to the age of eighty-four. And she never left the temple, serving night and day with fastings and prayers. *And at that very moment she came up and began giving thanks to God, and continued to speak of Him to all those who were looking for the redemption of Jerusalem.*
(Luke 2:36)

"That very moment" was the moment when Simeon blessed Jesus and His parents at the time of His circumcision, amazing them with the declaration that this child would be "a light of revelation to the Gentiles, and a glory to Thy people Israel" (Luke 2:32).

Women were not excluded from instructing.

Now a certain Jew named Apollos, an Alexandrian by birth, an eloquent man, came to Ephesus; and he was mighty in the Scriptures. This man had been instructed in the way of the Lord; and being fervent in spirit, he was speaking and teaching accurately the things concerning Jesus, being acquainted only with the baptism of John; and he began to speak out boldly in the synagogue. But when Priscilla and Aquila heard him, *they* took him aside and explained to him the way of God more accurately.   (Acts 18:24-26)

Observe that Paul is clearly saying that Priscilla taught a man more accurately concerning the Word. Notice also that Priscilla is mentioned first. In the protocol of the Bible, this means that Priscilla was a leader in their ministry as a team.

Paul speaks of MUTUAL authority in husband/wife relationships.

The wife does not have authority over her own body, but the husband does; and likewise also the husband does not have authority over his own body, but the wife does.   (1 Cor. 7:4)

Paul also speaks of MUTUAL sanctification.

The unbelieving husband is sanctified through his wife, and the unbelieving wife is sanctified through her believing husband; for otherwise are your children unclean, but now they are holy.(1 Cor. 7:14)

And he speaks of CORPORATE belonging.

We are members of His body.   (Eph. 5:30)

FOR THIS CAUSE A MAN SHALL LEAVE HIS FATHER AND MOTHER AND SHALL CLEAVE TO HIS WIFE; AND THE TWO SHALL BECOME ONE FLESH.(Eph. 5:31, Gen. 2:24)

WE ARE FELLOW CITIZENS WITH THE SAINTS, AND ARE OF GOD'S HOUSEHOLD,

having been built upon the foundation of the apostles and prophets, Christ Jesus Himself being the cornerstone, in whom the *whole* building, being fitted *together* is growing into a holy temple in the Lord; in whom you also are being built *together* into a dwelling of God in the Spirit. (Eph. 2:19-22)

This is God's perfect plan for all of us, that *together* we may truly become the Church through whom the manifold wisdom of God will be made known even to the rulers and authorities in the heavenly places. (See Eph. 3:10).

For us to participate in what God *will* accomplish, our petty pecking orders must die, along with all our anxious scrambling for recognition and position. Our needs to control our lives and the lives of others and to defend or exalt ourselves at the expense of others must die. Male and female, we must find our identity, worth and purpose first in the Lord Jesus.

There are no second-class citizens in the Kingdom of God. We are fellow citizens in His household. Let Him heal your wounds, forgive your sins, dispel your fears, sort out your confusions, and reveal to you the glory that you *are* in Him. Once that reality has been established in your heart, no one will be able to take it from you.

3
Learning to Live With Feelings

Everybody Has Feelings. Sometimes They Are Our Blessings, Sometimes Afflictions.

Some feelings are like embracing currents of light, fresh air which lifts and carries us to joyful and exciting heights. Others are oppressive mountains of heaviness, pressing and flattening even the innermost parts of us to the point of despair until pain gives way to numbness.

We have the capacity to feel wonderfully full to the point of explosion — full of gratitude, bursting with love, eight-and-a-half-months pregnant with expectation, overwhelmed with indescribable "wows!"; or we can feel so overcome with anger and frustration that the least stimulus is enough to blow the lid off our accumulated steam.

Common feelings find varieties of expression, often not understood.
Tears are a natural and healthy emotional release.

All of us, male or female, have experienced some degree of hurt, anger, disappointment, grief, and sorrow. Perhaps unhealed pain has multiplied within you, and your capacity to contain it has been strained

37

to the breaking point. You have felt uncomfortably pressured from within, and disoriented. Finally, tears have leaked uncontrollably through cracks in fleshly armor. And you have been embarrassed, fearful of being out of control, feeling guilty for seeming not to be "strong," not recognizing that God has created a safety valve in us and blessed healing release through tears.

Perhaps a loved one unwittingly has put you down by pressuring you to "pull yourself together." Or someone with misguided zeal may have knocked you into an emotional hole with heavy exhortations to "cheer up" or "have faith," when your weeping had nothing to do with a lack of faith, nor was it yet time to rejoice. And you have felt misunderstood, condemned, angry and disgruntled with people in general, and with yourself for your responses. Miserable, you have wrapped the darkness around you, not even wanting to come out. Hiding seemed to offer more comfort than being hit again.

Jesus Wept.

Jesus was "deeply moved in spirit and . . . troubled" (John 11:33) as He identified with those whom He found weeping over Lazarus' death, and He himself wept (John 11:35). He did not rush in, announcing He was going to raise Lazarus from the dead. Nor did He reprove the people. He entered into their sorrow and participated with them before He performed the miracle of resurrection He had planned beforehand. He is still doing that today as He bears our griefs and carries our sorrows (Isa. 53:4), as He comforts us, and calls us to do as He has done.

> Blessed be the God and Father of our Lord Jesus Christ, the Father of mercies and God of all comfort; who comforts us in all our affliction so that we may be able to comfort those who are in any affliction with comfort with which we ourselves are comforted by God . . . our comfort is abundant through Christ.   (2 Cor. 1:35)

> Rejoice with those who rejoice and weep with those who weep.   (Rom. 12:15)

Tears Are Not a Sign of Weakness.

I encourage you to let the tears flow when you have something to cry about, and not to believe anyone who tells you that grief and sorrow are a sign of lack of faith or a work of the devil. The ability to cry is a gift of God. Those who receive that gift and allow it to work in them appropriately are much less likely to suffer from high blood pressure, ulcers, nervous breakdowns, or depression than those who suppress and control their emotions to put forward a courageous front.

Most women seem to be able to cry more easily than most men. I don't believe this has anything at all to do with weakness. It has a great deal to do with permission given by our culture from the time we were children. Most of us, as little girls, didn't receive the repeated messages that little boys did: "Don't be a cry-baby." "Sissies cry." "When are you going to act like a man?"

Suppressed Tears May Come Up in Twisted, Embarrassing, and Even Hurtful Guise.

Most men have tender emotions, though many try to deny it, and they need to learn that it is not only okay, but very healthy to express themselves with tears. My husband was proud of his native American ancestry and vividly remembers his mother telling him, "Osage Indian boys don't cry." That message was strongly reinforced by strains of stoicism and reserve inherited through English streams in his family.

Added to these influences was the presence of strong defensive walls he had built to keep from being vulnerable to criticism and ridicule. Therefore, "don't cry" so powerfully influenced his sense of who he was, and was so integrally structured into his automatic response system, that it created problems, especially for me.

John was gifted with an extremely sensitive spirit. He could easily tune in to the upsets and hurts of others. But if he felt any inclination to weep for or with them, the programing in the computer of his heart automatically set him to respond defensively in one or both of two modes: (1) turn off or (2) laugh. It didn't bother me when he would laugh at a tear-jerker movie. Strangers sitting nearby often thought he was weird, but probably we would never see them again.

I was embarrassed and anxious, however, on one occasion when John laughed at a man who took an awkward fall over his dog's leash in the park. Granted, it was a comical sight but he could have been hurt, and that was also a part of John's perception, hence, his need to vent his emotions in his unusual way. The man was so angry at John's outward reaction that he actually started toward him to punch him, and was stopped only by a sincere and profuse apology from my husband.

The real problems were much deeper. There were times when I needed to spill out my hurt and frustration by crying. In those moments I was not seeking advice or counsel from anyone, especially not my husband. All I wanted was a warm, strong shoulder to cry on — someone to accept and meet me in my mess and love me to balance again. It was crushing to receive his "turn off" or "laugh" messages. I would plead with him,

"John, listen to me. I don't want you to be my counselor. I just want you to hold me!" — "John, it's not funny!"

"I'm not laughing at you."

"Then why is your face looking like that?"

By then (the conversation being somewhat condensed here), the prickles of budding anger were beginning to emerge from within me, and I had given him an excuse for not coming near. For years I stewed in the heat of periodic angers and he cooled in the isolation of his cave, until together we discovered the roots in both of us which created the dynamic, and began to learn to confront and overcome the "enemy" in a joint effort.

Sometimes We Cry the Tears Another Can't Cry.

Another problem issuing from the "no cry" syndrome

was that early in our marriage John would assume such a load of people's emotions as he ministered in the parish that he couldn't release them fast enough. Without realizing what he was doing, he would come home and pick on me until I cried. It was so foundationally and securely built into John that a real man would not for any reason strike a woman, he never even came close to abusing me physically. Nor has he even raised his voice more than once or twice.

He was, rather, in our early years together, an expert on "home refrigeration" or the "soft put-down." Wives live within the kind of one-flesh relationship in which, choose it or not, we really do bear our husbands' burdens (Gal. 6:2).

And by the same token, husbands can experience emotional release through their wives. As my tears flowed, he would feel relieved. Then he would struggle with guilt for feeling good when I was so miserable. When he finally experienced enough healing and strength of spirit to do his own crying, it was marvelous to experience the calm river of peace that carried us both.

Sometimes We Are Afflicted by Our Spouse's Desire to Protect Us.

Often a husband has thought to protect his wife by never sharing his problems. Such "protection" only afflicts her. He hasn't known that his wife will feel the heaviness or upset in him, and bear his burden more stressfully with no name on it. She may so often bear his unidentified burdens that she may frequently be so unexplainably saddened and cry so easily that he thinks he has married someone emotionally immature or unstable.

Many wives have carried such weights for so long that it has seriously affected their health. Perhaps he can't share the details of a problem he is working on without breaking a valid responsibility regarding government or job security, or confidentiality. But if he will learn to acknowledge generally the presence of a problem, and invite her to pray with him for wisdom and confidence, protection and refreshment, he will bless her and lighten the load she is carrying for him.

Inability or Refusal to Deal Appropriately With Our Emotions Can Result in Violence to Those We Love.

We have counseled numerous cases of wife-beating in which the husband was horrified at what he had inflicted on the woman he dearly loved. "I don't know what came over me!"

In each case we explored his relationship with his mother and other primary female figures in his childhood to determine what long-suppressed hurts, angers and frustrations he might now be unconsciously projecting onto his wife. Often this was a significant factor. He had suffered some sort of mental, emotional or physical abuse as a child. Overt reaction had only brought more abuse, so he had developed habitual ways of avoiding conflict and of suppressing his feelings until often they were hidden — even from himself.

Sometimes we found no history of abuse, but rather a family upbringing in which emotional issues were never discussed, thus never resolved. As a sensitive boy, one counselee had absorbed quantities of unexpressed and unidentified energies. He couldn't distinguish his own feelings from what he sensed from deep levels in others; he didn't even know it was possible to empathize involuntarily with others. But the undercurrent emotions of people had accumulated in his heart until he was like a land mine waiting to be stepped on.

Years later a conflict developed at work. Because it seemed insignificant at the time, and because he had never developed skills of recognizing, acknowledging and disciplining his own feelings, he characteristically ignored or suppressed them. He didn't know he was already fueled to the limit with combustible material.

Then he came home to his wife who "stepped" on him with words as innocent as a reminder that he had forgotten to carry out the trash. Powie!!!! The land mine exploded at her!

Sometimes we have found that an abusive husband is simply one who has swallowed the lie that a *strong* man *must* handle his own problems. He has struggled to do this until the load is so overpoweringly heavy it overcomes him. He drops it lest it crush him, and lashes out, blindly objectifying his desperation and anger on his wife, children, the dog, or inanimate objects — anyone or anything near at hand.

If you have been the recipient of abusive behavior, please hear this:

1. **You did not cause your husband to beat you.** It may be true that you have made judgments on men that they will act that way because you grew up in an abusive situation. You may still have some forgiving to do. Your expectations and your behavior may need some radical changing. But your husband must take *full* responsibility for his own sinful actions and reactions. He made choices, consciously or unconsciously, for which he is accountable. You are called to deal only with *your* sin.

2. **You cannot save or change your husband.** That is not your job. Only Jesus himself is big enough to transform lives. The goodness of your love may threaten him, because it makes him feel vulnerable, and vulnerability can be a fearful thing. The sweetness of your love alone, the more it melts his heart, may force him to insulate himself, or do something mean to cause you to back off. The power and wisdom of Jesus' love can eventually give him strength of spirit to admit his need and seek help.

Pray that the eyes of his heart be enlightened (Eph. 1:18), that he be strengthened in his spirit (Eph. 3:16), and continue to love him as best you can. But don't delude yourself into thinking that if you just love him enough he will be all right. He needs Jesus' love, and he needs a counselor who can objectively help him to get at the roots of his behavior. You are the least equipped to be objective because you are too emotionally risked with him.

3. **You are not called by anyone, least of all by God, to offer yourself as a punching bag.** Do not listen to the "religious" voices who tell you that you must take whatever comes in order to be a submissive wife. That is a totally warped interpretation of Scripture (see Chapter Two, "Women's Liberation in the Bible").

You are a child of God, His treasure, and you honor Him by esteeming yourself enough in Him to say to an abusive husband, "Your behavior is not acceptable, and I will not allow it because I value my life, and because I love you too much to let you continue in this pattern. *I will not enable you* to sow more and more negative seeds that you will eventually reap. Either get the help you need, or get out!" Many times, a temporary legal separation has provided the incentive for a reluctant husband to pursue the help he needs, and marriages have been restored to a healthy basis.

4. **Make sure your husband goes to a counselor of your choice.** Men left alone often choose counselors they can con — and no lasting healing results.

5. **Seek help yourself, preferably from a competent Christian counselor, and become part of a support group.** You have a life to live whether your husband responds or not. You need to deal with whatever may be in your heart which could draw more abuse to you.

6. **Do not confuse tears with repentance.** Watch for "fruit" in his life "in keeping with repentance" (Matt. 3:8, Acts 26:20). Let the counselor tell you when healing has progressed far enough to enable you to be safely together. Else the same pattern will repeat itself again and again.

Rivers of Tears Need Banks, and Rechanneling, Lest You Drown in an Undisciplined Flood.

I caution you that when you have allowed tears to accomplish their initial tension-releasing, cleansing effect, it is important to turn your attention outward to the concerns of others, lest you build retaining walls of self-pity and drown in the accumulating saltwater. Even before I specifically invited Jesus to crucify my habits of wallowing in feelings, of private speech-making and of self-pity, I knew I had to focus my rising energies of hurt and anger as aggressively and positively as I could, or my own fires would consume me. I knew discernment could be warped.

One small incident could be blown up to represent falsely the whole of our marital relationship and trap me in a lie that could become a prison. Or it might express itself like a knife going through me in criticism. An athletic morning of housecleaning or yard work, or a vigorous bike ride or walk with the children was often effective for me as a tension-releaser. A paint brush in my hand was an instrument of therapy as well as creativity. The paint stayed where I put it, and looked back at me as something beautiful and comforting.

But finding positive outlets for energies was seldom enough. I discovered that if I didn't discipline my thoughts, I could sometimes make up brilliant and increasingly angry speeches to the rhythm of my vacuum cleaner. When I tried to discipline my thoughts in the strength of my own flesh, I wearied myself and lost the battle. So I learned to pray simple, straightforward prayers at the moment I first recognized negative feelings rising in me. An example of such a prayer follows:

> Lord, I'm angry. I feel like punching him.
>
> I *feel* like I'm right and he's wrong, but I don't *know* that.
>
> Right or wrong, I'm responsible for my feelings, and what I do with them.
>
> I don't know how to change my feelings. But I choose not to entertain them or feed them (else they'll grow).I choose not to push them down (they'll come back up bigger and stronger).
>
> Here they are. Take charge of them and me.
>
> Give me *your* mind, *your* heart, *your* feelings, *your* response.
>
> P.S. Bless him.

Then I would go about my business. And God was faithful to do His part. Somewhere in the process, I learned to take personal responsibility for *my* sin, and *not* to take personally *every* hurtful word or action that came my way.

Let Nothing Terrify You.

There are many passages in the Bible which call us to live in a way that seems extremely difficult and often nearly impossible in the midst of a sinful generation. Not the least of these is First Peter 3. Married women are encouraged to live in a respectful relationship with their husbands:

> . . . So that even if any of them are disobedient to the word, they may be won without a word by the behavior of their wives, as they observe your chaste and respectful behavior. And let not your adornment be *merely* external — braiding the hair, and wearing gold jewelry, or putting on dresses; but let it be the hidden person of the heart, with the imperishable quality of a gentle and quiet spirit, which is precious in the sight of God. For in this way in former times the holy women also, who hoped in God, used to adorn themselves, being submissive to their own husbands. Thus Sarah obeyed Abraham, calling him lord, and you have become her children *if you do what is right without being frightened by any fear.*   (1 Peter 3:1-6)

The Amplified version translates the latter portion of that passage, ". . . if you do right and let nothing terrify you — not giving way to hysterical fears or letting anxieties unnerve you." What anxieties are there to unnerve a woman? What is there to terrify her? Paul is not talking to a specific category of battered and abused wives. He is addressing married women in general.

When Your Mate Has a Stony Heart.

Genesis 3:16 tells us that a woman's desire shall be for her husband. This does not refer only to sexual need or desire for security, protection and prestige. Far more important is her passionate desire to be for him all that she was created to be. She is bone of his bone and flesh of his flesh (Gen. 2:23), a joint-heir with him of the grace of life (God's unmerited favor — First Peter 3:7). She is the *one* God has provided to nurture and protect his heart (Prov. 31:11). He is the *one* God has provided to be primary human nurture and protection for her.

If her husband has been so wounded in his childhood that he has built and reinforced self-protective walls and self-centered coping mechanisms to defend himself — if he has developed a heart of stone (Ezek. 36:26 and 11:19) to avoid feeling pain, she is shut out. She feels rejected and undefended. More importantly, she isn't allowed to do what she instinctively knows she is designed and called to do, which is to be a comfort to him.

A wall is a wall, and it prevents the good as well as the bad from penetrating. Each time she reaches out to her husband and hits the hard walls of his heart, the more rejected and hopeless she feels. The more frustrated, anxious and perhaps even frantic she becomes. As she continues to fail in her attempts to break through, she even questions her own worth. The loneliness she lives with is often felt more keenly in his presence than away from him.

If a stony-hearted husband communicates at all, it is usually about superficial or peripheral matters. Or like a turtle he pops out periodically to test the atmosphere and withdraws quickly into his shell. He diligently avoids vulnerability. Though he may appear on the surface to be kind and giving, he is unable to receive more than carefully controlled tidbits from others.

His wife may live in excruciating loneliness, and even struggle with jealousy as she sees her husband relate easily and considerately with secondary people while she forever waits outside his door. Tragically, he may be totally unaware of his flight from corporateness, and deaf to the true meaning of her pleas as he tells his nagging wife, "Get off my back," or as he relaxes in the silence of her depression.

I am not now talking about the man who has only lost his ability to express his own emotions, nor the one who thinks to protect his wife by not sharing his troubles. I am describing a condition of much more serious bondage to fear and compulsion to control.

A person with a hardened heart may rationalize his own behavior and totally reject responsibility for having elicited negative responses from others. The harder his heart becomes, the more he loses awareness of the effect he has on people close to him, and perceives their attempts to break through to him as some form of criticism or attack.

Very early in John's life he lived with lacerating criticism. He learned that to find peace he had several alternatives. He could disappear from his home and run off to the barn or into the pasture to enjoy non-threatening fellowship with his dog, Joy, and his cow, Spring. They never talked back to him, and he could find easy rest and refreshment in their adoring company. He could also hide in the wonderful solitude of the attic and become lost in a book, or he could immerse himself in music.

Often it wasn't possible to disappear, so he developed an efficient skill of tuning out the critical voice of his mother in her presence. This ability, practiced over a long period of time, made it very easy for him to flee quickly into comfortable isolation without even thinking about it.

In the earlier years of our marriage, if challenging strains of "Why.....?" "Where.....?" — "Come here...." — "Will you?" — "Have you.....?" — "Are you listening?" (with or without critical overtones) began to fill the air, he was very quickly "gone."

There was rarely anything deliberate about that dynamic. It happened because it had been built in during his formative years and was automatically being projected onto his number-one primary person in the present — me. Of course, the yet-undealt-with areas of my own sinful nature fairly often made a significant contribution to the continuation of John's flight patterns.

Long-practiced habits eventually become automatic and compulsive. What has begun as a coping mechanism and a defense for emotional survival can and usually does become a prison. Jesus Christ came to set the prisoners free. Learning to receive, take hold of and live in that freedom is a process.

For many years John and I taught what we had learned concerning the heart of stone. John forgave those who needed forgiveness again and again, asked forgiveness for his own heart of stone, and prayed uncounted times that it be melted.

The Lord transformed many areas of my life also. Yet we became aware that there was a destructive pattern still operating in our lives. Often when everything had been going unusually well between us — we had enjoyed working together, had been refreshed by fun and recreation, had shared a particularly good sexual time with one another — John would manage within a day or two to do something mean and ornery. I would react with hurt and tearful anger. "What did I do? I thought everything was going great!" It didn't make sense to either one of us.

Then the Lord revealed that there were deeper levels of fear of vulnerability in John than we had yet seen. He could handle anything that appeared as an attack. He had built a sturdy defense against that, and a hiding place.

But when goodness, tenderness and sweetness began to melt the innermost core of his heart, he felt out of control. He had to do something to stop the flow of love. Then, if I retaliated with defensiveness, anger or accusation, he felt justified in withdrawing.

We talked and prayed about the problem together. We prayed that every demand-level and every need to control that existed in either of us be brought to death. I disciplined myself to learn better how to stop my anxious thoughts and take authority over my feelings by telling God about them, and by praying instantly for my negative reactions to be crucified. I also learned to resist the tendency to lick my wounds, and instead, spend that energy praying for John to be blessed with strength of spirit to hold his heart open. John learned better how to check his fears and rising impulses to flee, and to begin to take authority over his feelings and to pray, "Lord, keep me truly vulnerable."

Healing, transformation, and the melting of a stony heart are all part of a process. John thought this work in himself was finally completed. Then one evening at our kinship group he asked for prayer. He had some needs, and he was also setting an example of vulnerability for the others. Shortly into the prayer time, the group stopped to confront John in love. "John, why is it that when you ask us to pray for you, you very quickly turn the tables on us and start teaching us how, and how much, to minister to you?"

The old issue of fear and the need to control was dealt with again on another level as he forgave his mother

— AGAIN — and received forgiveness for his judgments and resultant coping mechanisms. The group prayed AGAIN that the old habits would die. John considered them to be dead and consequently brought forth a good deal of fruit that would indicate that it was so.

Several years later the same problem began to rise in different guises. John and I would be on the phone talking with our grown children. The conversations were pleasant, even delightful, but after a short time John would become uneasy and would excuse himself. He had something "important" to do and couldn't talk any longer.

After a few minutes, I would hear a toilet flush and the TV go on. I'd try to check my rising irritation, and would compensate for his absence by talking all the more enthusiastically with the children. Then I would confront him later about it, asking, "Why? Why?" He would come up with excuses which the Lord let him know were "too noble," and he had to face the truth again. The loving conversations were melting deeper levels of his heart of stone. He was fleeing from vulnerability.

By this time he had experienced enough healing and received enough strength of spirit that he could take full responsibility for his unconscious choices, and reckon the root of the sinful structure dead in himself. Is it finished? It was finished when Christ died on the cross for our sin.

Has John finished taking hold of what Christ accomplished for him? I don't know. But I sincerely and gratefully declare that our relationship is rich, growing, fulfilling, often exciting and generally peaceful. We are *together* and at rest because we are united in the power of the Lord against a common enemy, our own flesh (and the devil as he tries from time to time to expand whatever areas of sin we may try to hang onto). We are no longer fighting each other, and the Lord has transformed our struggles of the past to become part of our compassion, wisdom and gratitude for one another.

When Your Mate Cannot Be Trusted or Respected.

Far more hurtful than trying to share your life with a man who has a heart of stone, is a marriage where you are daily risking your life with a man who has no moral backbone, no real sense of integrity and truth, no stability or faithfulness in which you can rest.

However painfully intense John and I were in our problem solving, we never doubted one another's faithfulness, or loyalty or morality. Nor did we question the *intention* of the other to be honest and considerate. I could still respect my husband as being one after God's own heart even when he was in his late-bloomer stage, when he was running from the spectre of mother to his cave, when he was searching down blind alleys for truth, when he was not hearing or heeding me as I thought he should, and when he appeared to be controlling and critical. I even respected him during those times when I didn't feel loved and was aggressively angry and defensive; I didn't really want to be able to run him into the ground, and was relieved when he wouldn't let me.

Many women today are married to boys who have never grown up emotionally, and perhaps never will. These men come from dysfunctional families where basic trust was never established by clean, wholesome, affectionate touch and consistent, loving discipline. They are the shattered products of scattered families, a wounded generation which tends to seek comfort in drugs and alcohol and the accumulation of material wealth.

Multitudes struggle today in the midst of a confused generation which has lost the sense of the absoluteness of God's eternal laws. Whatever feels good must be okay, and only the "bigots" talk about what is wrong and right. They are a generation which has been well indoctrinated with demands for rights rather than taught about duties and responsibilities — a self-seeking generation in which few know the meaning of laying down their own lives for the sake of blessing others.

Of course, women are a part of that same generation, but in most cares, they are less out of touch with who they are. Our culture has done more to destroy the role of men than of women, though clearly female identity is also being threatened with demolition today. Very few men today have grown up working alongside their fathers as young men did in previous generations. Fathers are extremely rare who make themselves present to their children with quality time, and give affectionate attention and consistent appropriate discipline.

Therefore, sons have not had strong wholesome male role models with whom to identify. Mothers are important, and a boy's identification with her is from the womb. But if the father is not there for him in a way that communicates security and belonging, he cannot with restful confidence move from the familiarity of his mother to embrace a world away from her.

A little boy especially needs to develop a secure relationship and identification with his father as he notices that his sexual equipment is not like that of his mother and begins to separate from her by virtue of his differentness. If the father/son relationship is not well-built (or if he does not have a relationship with another primary male figure), then male identification is difficult and his sense of who he is becomes confusing. Women don't have to make that sort of transition. From their conception on, they remain identified with their femaleness (unless some trauma disrupts their lives and causes them to reject their identity with mother).

Though multitudes of today's young men have been denied strong father models, they have had abundant opportunity to feed on the modeling of the TV "hero" who jumps into bed with every female he dates even casually. He has grown up with exaltation of the macho figure who never expresses a real emotion about anything. He has learned to cheer for the clever and often-charming criminal who gets away with his crime, and a suitcase of money and the gorgeous lady, and in the process makes a fool of a whole battalion of officers in a chase that wrecks dozens of police vehicles.

He has witnessed murder and rape to the point of being desensitized to the horror of it. Pornography is represented as being "adult," condoms as guaranteeing "safe" sex, and reaching the age of twenty-one as being "mature" enough to go out to get drunk. For those who are in a hurry to "grow up," all of these things, plus varieties of drugs, are fairly easily available to schoolchildren.

Who will tell our young men the truth about what it is to be a man? Who will model manhood to them so that they can know what it is to be a husband and a father? Who will give them strength of spirit to stand against the destructive forces in our culture? Who will awaken conscience in them? Who will teach them what love actually is? The Holy Spirit has been falling on many people in what has been the sleeping giant, the Church, calling them to the task.

Meanwhile, it is a scary business in countless cases for a woman to trust herself to be joined to a man, to submit her life to him, to become one flesh with him, if, for example, she knows he has been with many women before, is still temptable, and has no conscience about it. She worries that he may show up at some time testing HIV positive. She feels continually defiled. What is she to do?

Similarly, how can she respect her husband if she knows he is not dealing honestly in business? That he is wasting their resources and not paying bills? How can she truly meet him in their relationship when his sensitivities are dulled by alcohol and/or drugs? How can she even talk with him about these things when she has cause to be afraid of his responses?

In the beginning Abraham apparently was not wise, mature and considerate in relation to his wife, Sarah. He lied to King Abimelech, saying she was his sister, and the king took her into his own house. For fear that he himself might be killed, Abraham deliberately put his wife in a position where she could have been forced into adultery.

At that point in his life Abraham was certainly not a husband who would risk himself to protect his wife. And yet Sarah obeyed him. God himself protected Sarah, did not allow the king to touch her, and then rebuked Abimelech and Abraham (Gen. 20). The same scenario was repeated in Genesis 26 with Isaac, Rebekah and Abimelech.

I interpret Peter's words, "You have become her children if you do right and let nothing terrify you," to mean that women, like Sarah, can dare to give themselves into the care of an immature, self-centered, untrustworthy husband, only if they have developed a strong enough relationship with God.

Too many women expect too much from their husbands and lean too heavily on them, asking them to do what only God can do. "It is better to take refuge in the LORD than to trust in man. It is better to take refuge in the LORD than to trust in princes" — (Ps. 118:9). "Do not trust in princes, in mortal man, in whom there is no salvation" (Ps. 146:3).

Every man (and woman) is an arm of flesh, and an arm of flesh will fail you at some time or another. Only God himself can be trusted to relate to us perfectly. God alone is able to sort out a husband's errors, rebuke him appropriately and redeem the effects of sin.

There is no guarantee that a woman's husband will ever change, even if her behavior reflects the righteousness of God and though she may have all the faith in the world. God moves powerfully upon the hearts of His children but never forces anyone to receive anything. Therefore, a woman needs to develop her own strength and power in a growing relationship with the Lord so as to know who she is and how to stand.

If her strength is first of all in God, she can then be appropriately dependent on her husband and at the same time properly independent. Jesus says, "If anyone comes to Me, and does not hate his own father and mother and wife [or husband] and children and brothers and sisters, yes, and even his own life, he cannot be My disciple" (Luke 14:26). Of course Jesus does not call us to *hate* in the sense of strong destructive emotions directed toward people. He has called us to love even our enemies.

What He calls us to hate is the continuing carnal influence and fleshly ties and loyalties which keep us from giving Him first place in our lives. As we cut free from emotional bondages and learn to follow Jesus, we are enabled to love as He loves and see ourselves and others as He sees.

Develop Sources of Refreshment Which Are Not Dependent on Your Husband.

A woman must develop some sources of refreshment which are not dependent on her husband so as to have strength to keep going back to him. She needs the fellowship of a few close friends with whom she can talk and laugh and cry, people who share common interests with her and know how to play and enjoy life.

She will benefit greatly from regular exercise, music and good books. It is healthy for her to take some time to develop her special skills, whatever they may be — sewing, art, crafts, writing, some sort of job. . . . And ideally she should be grounded in the nurturing and supportive fellowship of some sort of kinship group in a church of good Christian faith. It is wisdom to avoid scheduling personal refreshment resources at times which would conflict with her husband's need to be with her, lest he jealously react to these as competition.

What Are We To Do With Fears and Feelings?

What are we to do with our fears and feelings? How are we to avoid giving way to hysterical fears, not letting anxieties unnerve us?

Cast your burden upon the LORD, and He will sustain you; He will never allow the righteous to be shaken.   (Ps. 55:22)

Your necessary righteous discipline is to cast your burden on the Lord when you first become aware of it, before it has the opportunity to take firm hold of you. Don't entertain it. Don't wallow in it. Don't feed it with resentment and bitterness. Acknowledge it, offer it to the Lord, release it, affirm your identity in Him, and go about your business.

4

A TIME FOR GRIEF AND SORROW

There is a *time* for every event under heaven —
... A *time* to weep, and a *time* to laugh; A *time*
to mourn, and a *time* to dance.   (Eccles. 3:1,4)

Grief may last a long time when we lose someone
we care about — especially one who has never known
the Lord. To receive comfort from Jesus in such a case
involves repeated choices to lay down our fears,
judgments and unanswered questions. It means trusting
in God's ability to run His universe in love and justice
and mercy.

Grief may be quickly healed following the loss of
loved ones who you know have gone to be with the
Lord. You have wept for them, and now you rejoice
for them. You have faith to believe that someday you
will be reunited with them. Yet sorrow may surge up
into tears at unexpected times when memories are
triggered or treasured new events happen in your life
which you can share with your loved one no more.
Those tears are a natural, healthy reaction, nothing to
be ashamed of. Let them flow. Tell the Lord about your
feelings, and go on about your business. Don't try to

suppress feelings; volcanos are built that way.

Let me share from my own experience with grief and sorrow.

When a Parent Dies.

My father was a hero figure in my life. His job required him to travel a great deal, but when he came home to his family, he was one hundred percent with us. I was the oldest of five children, and we always anticipated his Friday homecomings. We would wait excitedly for him to walk through the door with that familiar grin on his face, his arms outstretched to share hugs. Mother would come out of the kitchen to greet him warmly, then scurry back to finish dinner preparations.

Often he would waltz along behind her to tease her lovingly with ridiculous humor, especially if he sensed that she was weary and uptight from the accumulated burdens of her solo time with the likes of us. Soon he would have her laughing. After dinner the two of them would sit down at the piano to fill the house with music — she at the keyboard and he with his clarinet — and we would often join in with singing.

Before Saturday was over he had inquired about our school adventures and misadventures, mediated occasionally in unfinished conflicts, fixed whatever broken things there were around the house, and shared himself where we had need (sometimes even getting onto stilts, skates or scooters with us when we were young).

On Sundays we all went to church together, and in the afternoon dad would load us all into the car to take us on exploratory trips around St. Louis and the surrounding countryside. Driving the car again was the last thing a traveling salesman wanted to do, but he knew we loved it. The crowning point of each adventure was that we were given the privilege of choosing what delicious thing we each wanted to buy with our five cents. In Depression and post-Depression days, this was luxury!

On Sunday evenings dad always had to spend time typing his job reports before leaving the next morning. He didn't need a calculator; he added figures in his head more quickly and easily. Though he had never studied algebra, he sometimes helped me with my homework. He could solve a difficult problem with simple arithmetic, and explain it so clearly that I could then easily translate the process into algebraic terms.

He never seemed to be upset when we interrupted his typing. When we asked him a question, he would slowly look up from his work with his dentures hanging out the corner of his mouth for our amusement, and with a twinkle in his quizzical eyes, ask, "What now?" If we came crashing by in an argumentative or rambunctious hassle, he would settle the disturbance with a justly stern but quiet reprimand we knew we deserved.

Mother had to be the principal disciplinarian because she was home with us full-time, and it sometimes got to be a bit too much for her emotions to handle. But he was a calm, consistent, solid support beneath her, and we knew it.

My parents retired at the same time, he from sales and she from teaching, and spent a number of years doing many things they hadn't been able to do together when dad was traveling and mom was too busy keeping the home-front in healthy order. They gardened, traveled, made calls for the church on newcomers and shut-ins, signed up for classes in oil painting and tole art, put in volunteer time in the Missouri Baptist Hospital gift shop, took long walks in the evening hours, and made close friends of their neighbors.

It was excruciating for all of us when dad developed Alzheimer's disease. We watched helplessly as the lovable and dependable rock we had known slowly cracked and crumbled. Dad began to be disoriented at times. The man who had always known how to get where he was going would suddenly find himself lost in familiar places and have to ask for help in order to get home. That was bewildering and humiliating for him.

He had always been top salesman for his company, largely because of his ability to communicate ideas as well as charming integrity. Now, simple words would suddenly be lost from his vocabulary, and he would stop in the middle of a sentence, not knowing what to say, a furtive look rising in his eyes as he struggled to get hold of the right word for articles as common as "table" and "bread."

When it first began to happen, if we could supply the missing word, his eyes would brighten and he would laugh as he continued. But he grew more and more frustrated in trying to express himself, and would sometimes quietly throw up his hands, as tears welled up in his eyes.

When the doctors diagnosed his problem as Alzheimer's disease, they offered no hope for recovery. It was extremely hurtful for him to have to give up driving, and humiliating when he had to surrender taking care of the checking account. He gradually lost track of time and would get out of bed at all hours of the night. Mom became afraid to go to sleep for fear he might wander outside. The simple functions of table utensils became a mystery to him, and he lost the ability to dress himself properly. But he never lost the desire to be helpful around the house, and persisted in continually reorganizing things in strange ways and places.

Mom was exhausting herself, but determined that as long as her beloved husband was able to recognize people, she would take care of him at home. When she slipped and fell on the way to the mailbox and had to have surgery for a complete hip replacement, it seemed to us that God had intervened and taken the decision out of her hands.

My brother Jerry and sister Sue, whose homes were nearer than any of the rest of us, placed dad in an excellent Christian nursing home, explaining carefully to him what had happened, that mother was in the hospital and would be alright, but wasn't able to be home to care for him. He couldn't put it all together, but he did grasp with great anxiety that she had been injured. After she recovered and came to see him nearly every afternoon, he would embrace her, pat her gently, touch the walker that she used for a while, and strain with questions and concern for her that he couldn't put into words.

The nurses were unusually kind and affectionate. They quickly discerned that his humor was still alive, and would brighten his days by flirting and joking with him. Unfortunately, his desire to help was also still alive, so he quickly busied himself with the removal and rearrangement of the doorknobs in the Alzheimer patients' wing, and was totally dismayed when they put a firm halt to his project.

He was upset when they locked his belongings in the closet to protect them from other patients who would wander in and carry away whatever was available. "I don't have anything!" he cried. We brought him a little book with all the pictures of his family in it, and he carried it with him wherever he went. From the evidence of tears on some of the pages, I believe He wept over the photos at times. The staff again and again asked my mother, "Has he always been such a kind man? Usually these patients become belligerent! But Paul is always so kind!"

It is difficult to describe the feelings that beset me as I watched my father become more and more lost from himself and us. One day when I came to St. Louis to visit, we walked together up and down the corridor, arm in arm, again and again. His walk was a halting shuffle. But he saw a patient heading directly toward us in a wheelchair, and from somewhere inside this man who had been leaning heavily on me to keep his balance, came a momentary surge of strength — he pulled me out of the path of the wheelchair.

I was nearly overwhelmed — first, by the undying protective father-love in my dad — and, secondly, with the realization of the power of love within the human spirit to enable the mind and body to rise above physical limitations to accomplish impossible tasks.

When I left my father that day, we hugged each other for a long time, cried together, and I told him how precious he was, how much we all loved him and how proud I was of him. He walked with me as far as the fence which separated the patients from the elevator door, quietly smiled through his tears, and watched with deep sadness in his eyes as I walked into the elevator. When the door shut, and no one was there, I collapsed into sobs.

It is a wonder that I made it to my parents' home safely through city traffic with no windshield wipers for the torrents flooding my eyeballs. I talked straight-turkey to God about my feelings — "I am so hurt for him — and so angry! He was so good — and he gave so much — and he finally had time to rest and enjoy life! He and mom had to be satisfied with weekend fellowship in their marriage for so many years! Why this? Why couldn't they live out the rest of their lives

together? They don't deserve this! It doesn't seem fair!"
I went on and on and on.

And God just listened. I knew He was hearing with
compassion. When I had poured out enough of the pain,
I prayed and continued to pray, "Lord, have mercy on
him. Please, will you either heal him completely, or take
him home to be with you? But I earnestly pray you
release his beautiful spirit from the prison of his
deteriorating mind and body. Let him know he hasn't
been abandoned here in this place. Take him into your
house, Lord, and into your arms, and wipe away all
his tears. Fill him with your healing love. Lord, he never
really knew what it was to have a father, and yet he
did a good job of fathering anyhow. Let him come into
his inheritance with you. Let him *know you,* Father, and
give him comfort and joy. Let him know how much
we all love him, and how much we appreciate the many
ways he laid down his life for us."

The more I cried and prayed, the better I felt. A peace
settled into my innermost being. Something inside of
me let go. I didn't strive emotionally anymore to make
something happen that was beyond my control. I didn't
have to wrestle with my feelings any longer, or with
guilts for things I had done or left undone in relation
to him as I was growing up. I wasn't plagued any longer
with unanswered questions.

I returned home to Idaho, into a busy ministry
schedule, and continued to send frequent picture-
postcards with simple bits of news and "I love you"
messages. I knew Dad's spirit could still understand and

needed the touch of my love again and again. And I prayed that God would comfort and nurture him in the depths of his spirit.

God answered my prayer. Later I learned that others in the family had been praying similarly. In a short time my father had a series of small strokes and went home to be with the Father. He didn't have to go through all the debilitating stages of Alzheimer's disease. He never lost his ability to recognize relatives and close friends who came to visit. He never completely lost his sense of humor. He never ceased to be kind.

We all wept at his passing, though not long. It was sweet sorrow, and the weeping was largely for us. Our dad was gone. We would miss him. Mostly we rejoiced for him; he had been let out of prison, set free to be and express those qualities with which he had blessed us for so many years — more uninhibitedly and purposefully than ever before.

Grief had been spent during the emotionally painful and seemingly endless days of my father's illness. It was overcome by the celebration of joy and gratitude for his being released to go to the Father. But apparently the Lord is still ministering to five-year-old residues of sweet sorrow. Last night as I typed this story, He drew tears again from somewhere in the hidden depths of me, and today I feel like I've had a holy and refreshing bath. Is that the end of it? I don't know, and I won't worry about it. That's God's business, and He knows my heart — for my good.

The adage that you can't teach an old dog new tricks did not apply to my aging mother. She not only grew more mellow in heart and flexible of mind, but younger and more vital in spirit as well as she grew older. Rather than settling down and stagnating in familiar ways of acting and controlling life, she sturdily maintained the best of her time-tested principles, but at the same time reached out to embrace the world of adventure and insight being introduced to her by her children. She wanted everything God wanted for her.

Very soon after my father died, she accompanied John, our daughter Andrea, and me, on a trip to Israel and five countries in Europe. She was wise enough to know she needed to fill her days with forward-looking, life-giving activities. In Israel our group did an unusual amount of walking and the hip replacement she had received gave her some discomfort, but she didn't want to miss anything.

The only hill she couldn't climb was the heights of Masada when we found the gondola broken, and she declined that challenge primarily because she didn't want to slow us down. She had grown accustomed to costing herself whatever pain was necessary in order to do what she counted joyous and important.

When we were children, mom suffered from severe varicose veins. In pre drip-dry and blow-dry days, everything had to be ironed. St. Louis could be hotter than Hades in summer, but morning after morning she would stand for hours, ironing till her basket was empty. Then she would gather us, and as many neighborhood children as possible, into our car, and take us to the zoo, or to see an auto assembly plant, an art museum, a packing plant, or a jam factory, trotting around with us on those aching legs.

I'm sure that as a child I didn't understand the full value of that gift, but as an adult I can now recognize that spirit of self-sacrifice with deep appreciation — and some guilt for taking so much for granted.

In her younger days, she didn't exhibit much of a sense of humor, and really needed dad to make her laugh. But in Europe as we traveled eighty-five mph in the slow lane on the Autobahn while Mercedes Benzes whipped by at plus-120, she scooted behind John in the driver's seat so she couldn't see the speedometer, and chanted, "Oh my-oh my-oh my-oh my . . ." We called her "Oh-my Bowman" and she laughed through her fears.

Two years ago mom came to visit at the time of our daughter Ami's wedding. She was excited and enthusiastic as she visited in the homes of all her grandchildren and great-grandchildren. She helped with the wedding preparations, decorating and making salad and sandwiches. She worked alongside the rest of us as we set up chairs for the reception, and delighted in visiting with all the guests. When she mentioned later that she was feeling a little tired, we suggested that she rest, but felt no undue concern. A much younger person would have had good reason to be weary. She revived and climaxed her visit with a wonderful time at a barbecue in our son Loren's back yard.

A week and a half after she returned home, she died of acute leukemia! Even the doctor did not suspect anything serious, and at first had only treated her at home for what he thought were merely flu symptoms. When she became too exhausted to talk on the telephone, my sister took her to the hospital.

John and I were in Winnipeg, Canada, at a TV station making a series of videos. We received a call that carried with it the assurance that mom's condition was improving. We finished the videos in an afternoon marathon and then John flew to a conference in Dallas where we were scheduled to speak; I flew on to St. Louis to be with my mother, and with the rest of my family who had come from various parts of the United States.

Expecting to find her improved, I was shocked to find her in a comatose state. Two of my brothers shared that they believed she could hear us, that a little earlier in the day they had said to her that they were going to get some lunch. She had roused a moment, pointed to her purse, and said, "There's some money in there." That gesture had almost wiped them out — nearly comatose on her death-bed, she was still thinking of their welfare!

My brother Stan, from Florida, was the last to arrive at the hospital, and I said to our mother, "Every one of your children are here now, mom." She wasn't able to answer, but we all visited quietly, and in a very short while she let go, and was gone.

The nurse said, "Her vital signs were so weak I couldn't understand what was keeping her alive. She must have been waiting for you." We all sat in stunned silence. My brother Norman was kneeling at her bedside, and I believe we were all praying silently. But none of us was praying with any of the ease with which we usually had been able to pray for others.

I couldn't take hold of my thoughts. "O God — bless her" was all I could put together; I felt as if I could explode with emotion, but had no way to let it out. It was as if I were suspended helplessly. I desperately wanted to do something, and didn't know what it was or how to get hold of it.

We were, for a time, a unit of intense loneliness. Then we got up, hugged one another, and walked out silently, pausing for a moment to thank the nurse for her kindness to our mother. She replied, her eyes swimming with tears, "She ministered to me."

It was a quiet evening, and the Lord unplugged gushers of pent-up emotion in the privacy of our bedrooms. I was then easily able to pray blessing and release, and fell asleep with an awareness of the comforting presence of God.

The pastor came to visit, and asked simply that we tell him about our mother. We had a good time sharing the precious memories we had. Then the pastor told us some things we hadn't known. He was having to find a number of people to replace her in the life of the church.

At eighty-three, she had been teaching a Sunday school class for some fifteen or so shut-ins by conference call on the phone each Sunday morning for a half hour. She hadn't been satisfied with just talking to people she couldn't see, so she had driven all over St. Louis to meet each one of them personally! Once a month she taught one of the other adult classes at the church. She played the piano for the midweek meeting. In the senior citizen's choir she was the voice on whom the whole alto section relied. Often she would host visiting evangelists and teachers in her home.

This pastor had lived with her for three weeks when he first moved to St. Louis. Her home Bible study group was the only group in which people were really opening their hearts to give and receive personal ministry. He was trying to find someone to replace her as Bible study leader at an upcoming retreat at Green Lake, Wisconsin.

We all agreed that we had lived as though we expected her to live forever here, and we saw that she had been the glue that held our far-flung family together, as she so often wrote to all of us to tell us what everyone else was doing.

When my husband John first arrived for the funeral, and saw mom in the casket, he was puzzled. Then he realized why. In all the thirty-seven years we had been married, he had never seen her lying down. She was always busy serving others!

At her funeral, the pastor told what we had shared with him, and summed it all up, by reading the closing refrain of a poem I had written years before when my parents celebrated their fiftieth wedding anniversary:

Some plan and scheme and push as children grow —
And bind their offspring to them as they go
In selfish striving.
But mother launched her dreams from ironing boards,
And blessed their rising.

We all stayed for a few days, visiting together and dispensing household belongings so my sister would not have the whole burden of settling the estate. The first stages of grief had passed quickly. Sorrow was a strong undercurrent, but it could not overcome our sense of celebration. We all kept exclaiming, "It's so good to be together! Wouldn't mom and dad enjoy this!"

Someone said, "I'll bet dad is one especially happy guy today." We comforted one another with positive remarks about how glad we were that both parents had lived long, full lives, how wonderful it was that our mother's prayer never to be a burden to anyone was fulfilled, what a rich legacy we had been left, etc. Our conversation was a healing balm at the time, and we meant what we were saying — but it did not do away with what we would all find ourselves experiencing in the months to come.

John and I left within a week for a month-long trip to many churches in Scotland, Wales and England. I felt reasonably settled and comforted inside. My full attention was focused on the work at hand. Then our youngest daughter, Andrea, phoned us in Paisley, Scotland, to tell us that she and Randy were planning to be married at Christmas. I put the phone down and began to share the news excitedly with John.

But a sudden uprush of deep sorrow overwhelmed me and I delivered the joyful news through a stream of tears. I couldn't call my parents to tell them the good news about their granddaughter! I hadn't been aware of the emotion still needing release from deep inside of me. Later, near Lancaster, England, as John and I were walking alone beside a beautiful river, I experienced the same overwhelming flood. John comforted me and helped me realize that I had been so completely occupied with others' needs that I had neglected my own need to work through the process of grieving completely. We shared our mutual feelings of sorrow, and it felt good.

The Lord had used the quiet loveliness of that remote pastoral area to still my busy mind so He could minister healing to the depths of my spirit. I had buried my feelings of guilt for having been so emotionally paralyzed and prevented from audible prayer at my mother's death. At the rational level, I knew that there was nothing any of us *could* have done. But at the emotional level, I needed the assurance of forgiveness. Later, the sorrow arose with the joyful birth of each of three new grandbabies. By this time, however, I had learned what is comforting to me to do instantly with such feelings. It is so simple: "Jesus, I can't share the good news with them, but you can. Will you please deliver a message?"

When a Husband Dies.

It is natural to grieve and experience sorrow for a time after the death of an aging parent. But it is far more intense when a husband dies!

Hopefully, a daughter has individuated — which means that she has become her own person and has cut free emotionally from her parents in order to become truly one flesh with her husband (Gen. 2:24, Eph. 5:31, Ps. 45:10). A new quality of relationship in loving and caring for parents, free of childhood loyalties and dependencies, should have been established by then.

Of course, she will feel a great sense of loss when her parents die. But she should have already experienced as an adult, and further as a married woman, letting go of them as primary supporters, affirmers, protectors, providers, confidants and advisors. Her husband is more than primary *to* her; he is one flesh *with* her. Therefore, her parents' passing contains far less trauma than the loss of her husband.

When your husband dies, you feel torn apart. You were bone of his bone and flesh of his flesh (Gen. 2:23). You have shared intimacy to the degree of the blessedness of your marriage — mind to mind, heart to heart, body to body, spirit to spirit. All the spiritual faith and emotional strength in the world will not prevent your bleeding and your pain.

But on the other hand, "Blessed are those who mourn, for they *shall* be comforted" (Matt. 5:4). "He *heals* the brokenhearted and binds up their wounds" (Ps. 147:3). Emotional healing does not usually happen instantly. God respects your feelings, your need to grieve for a while. He knows your willingness to receive from Him, and your readiness to emotionally let go of a loved one and set your face forward to live. He longs to pour the balm of His Spirit into your wounds like a medicine, but He waits for your invitation.

> The *LORD longs to be gracious to you,* and therefore He waits on high to have compassion on you. For the LORD is a God of justice; how *blessed are all those who long for Him.* (Eph. 30:18)

Your prayer invitation is like turning on a faucet. The water pressure is already there; the water flows out to fill your cup when you turn on the tap. If you hold a full cup to the faucet and turn it on, at first it will not hold the water. If you persist in holding the cup there, soon what has been in your cup will be displaced by the steady pressure of the water flowing into it. It is the same with your grief.

If the cup of your innermost being is filled with grief, do not wait until you are free of grief to offer yourself to the Lord and turn the faucet of prayer. You may sit for a very long time with a cup you are unwilling or afraid to share with Him, and its contents will become bitter. Offer your cup as it is, now, and choose to trust

God to pour His water with the measure of power He knows is best for you.

It is commonly very difficult to pray while experiencing intense emotion. At such times, it has been comforting for me to read:

The Spirit also helps our weakness; for we do not know how to pray as we should, but *the Spirit Himself intercedes for us with groanings too deep for words;* and He who searches the hearts knows what the mind of the Spirit is, because He intercedes for the saints according to the will of God. (Rom. 8:26,27)

So I encourage you to relax, be, feel, open your heart to Jesus as best you can and choose to trust that God is ultimately in charge, and will cause all things to work together for good (Rom. 8:28).

Some within the Body of Christ have said that Christians should not grieve at all, and have quoted the following Scripture as their "proof" text:

But we do not want you to be uninformed, brethren, about those who are asleep, that you may not grieve, as do the rest who have no hope. For if we believe that Jesus died and rose again, even so God will bring with Him those who have fallen asleep in Jesus.   (1 Thess. 4:13,14)

This passage does not say we will not or should not grieve at all. Rather, it says that if we understand what the death and resurrection of Jesus means, we will not grieve in the same way as people do who have no hope in Jesus. We will experience pain as we are separated from those we love. But the substance of our hope is that we know we will someday be reunited with them in Him. Separation is temporary. Comfort is continually available.

Grief is soon healed by prayer. Sorrow will linger awhile. You may be cleaning a closet and find an old sweater of his — sudden tears surprise you. You put it on and wear it around the house awhile because it feels good. An advertisement comes in the mail, addressed to him. A wave of sadness hits you, and perhaps even a tiny flicker of anger. "Don't they know he's not here anymore?"

Thanksgiving and then Christmas arrive, and you sit down to enjoy a sumptuous meal with your family. You find yourself remembering past holidays when he was there at the head of the table, and for a moment you feel very lonely — even in the midst of loved ones. Such waves of sorrow are to be expected for a time. Don't be embarrassed or impatient with yourself when you experience them. Don't apologize for tears.

But neither should you allow your feelings to rule the day. Let your feelings live, acknowledging them silently to the Lord, giving Him charge over you. Then turn to focus on the joyful reason for the holiday, and pour yourself as best you can into fellowship with family and friends. Life continues on this planet, and God calls you to invest your life here as fully as possible until He calls you to leave.

Some make the mistake of trying to develop another primary relationship too soon after the death of a spouse. There is a hole inside which begs to be filled. There is an aching loneliness that nothing seems to comfort fully. There may be multitudes of practical household business details your husband used to take care of, and you took for granted — insurance, bills, car maintenance and repair, investments. Even though you may at first be intimidated, by the challenges you manage, with good counsel, to equip yourself with sufficient knowledge to cope. But you find it tremendously difficult and exhausting to live with the emptiness you feel. You can fill your days with busyness, but the nights are long, and TV can be depressing company.

Even if your relationship with God is good and vital, there are ways in which even He cannot satisfy you completely. You need love with skin on it. Touches and hugs.

Friends try to be there for you. They still invite you to group gatherings which used to mean so much to you and your husband. But he isn't there anymore, and the fellowship isn't the same. You appreciate the love of your friends, and their desire to include you, but you feel somehow awkward and undressed without him.

If you rush out to try to fill the vacuum with any but God's presence and the support of *friends* for a period of at least two years or more, until you are healed, you are likely to reap heartache. It will be extremely difficult to relate to a new mate with your whole being. You need time to cut free emotionally from whatever quality of one-fleshness you have experienced with your husband.

Memories will rise frequently. Especially if your marriage was a blessed and fulfilling one, it will be difficult to shed expectations formed by the familiar satisfying and comfortable ways blessing has come to you in the past. You could so easily, without intending, make comparisons that could fall as judgment and burden on a new and different spouse. Worse, such comparisons could be expressed unconsciously from hidden places in your heart.

Your familiar and practiced identifications of love need time to die. And a new relationship, if it is to have a healthy future, must develop from a base of mutual friendship and sharing rather than the pressures of need.

Cry your tears.

Take your quiet times to sort out memories; express your gratitudes, regrets, hurts, angers, fears and needs to the Lord — unpolished.

Invite Jesus' comfort and healing. Let Him love you.

Let others pray for you and with you.

Release your loved one to God the Father, in prayer.

Choose life.

Spend time doing things you have always enjoyed.

Seek the company of those with whom you feel comfortable.

Listen to music, whatever kind lifts your spirit.

Turn outward to help others.

Don't be dismayed when emotions rise from time to time. And don't be disturbed when people fail to understand. God knows your heart, and persists to draw your residue of sorrow to himself.

5

Guilt and Grief
Following the Loss of a Child

God's *perfect* plan is clearly expressed in the Word of
God:

Behold, children are a gift of the LORD; the fruit
of the womb is a reward. Like arrows in the hand
of a warrior, so are the children of one's youth.
How blessed is the *man* whose quiver is full of
them.   (Ps. 127:3)

I can remember reading those words years ago, and
thinking, *"Whose* quiver is full? Who is carrying all these
babies anyhow?" This was immediately after the birth
of our sixth child. Our older children, delighted with
the tiny golden-redhead who had just joined our family,
were already including as their contribution to our table
grace, "...and please, God, let mom have another
baby."

I told John I'd be happy to let him be pregnant with
number seven if God should decide to bless his quiver
again. Now I've written and read my chapter on
women's liberation in the Bible and understand that I
as a woman am also called "man." Now I know the
verse means that we both receive blessing. And we
have, in unbelievable measure, as our children have

followed in our spiritual footsteps, taking ever larger, faster and more gracefully productive steps than we ever did.

I have never lost a child, though I have experienced the anxiety of repeated threats of losing one. Loren entered this world in a drugged state because of ether the doctor gave me (without anyone's permission). Ami was conceived as a tubal pregnancy. Mark threatened for several weeks to miscarry. Johnny was born with an unusually long umbilical cord partially wrapped around his neck. And I had to stay in bed for six weeks to avoid miscarrying Tim.

When I was in labor with Andrea, and the doctor tried to break the water, there was none. Andrea slipped sideways, the cord was wrapped around her, and her heartbeat was fading. The doctor managed to turn her into proper position and literally *pull* her into the world safely. I am well acquainted with anxiety and fervent prayer, as well as relief and gratitude. I can identify with mothers who have lost their babies, because I know I would have been crushed if I had lost any one of ours, early or late. I know I would have wrestled intently with the questions, "What did I do wrong? What could I have done differently?"

Mothers Should Not Automatically Blame Themselves for Miscarriages.

Studies tell us that one in five pregnancies ends in a miscarriage. Three out of four miscarriages occur before the tenth week, and sometimes before the mother even realizes she is pregnant. It is natural for a woman to wonder if she is in some way responsible for a miscarriage. But guilt feelings are usually inappropriate.

Miscarriages do not happen because you had a fight with your husband, because you are over-tired, because you are upset about finances, or tense after a prolonged and difficult visit from your mother-in-law. Lots of noise and commotion in your household does not constitute enough of a bomb to blast the baby loose. And if the tiny, just-beginning baby is healthy and attached properly, you aren't going to cause it to detach simply by tripping over the rug and falling down.

There are natural, physical causes for most miscarriages.

Your doctor is not just trying to make you feel better when he tells you that miscarriage is nature's way of sloughing a defective embryo. He is telling you the truth. Some of the causes for early miscarriage are: fetal abnormalities that would not allow survival, fertilized eggs that do not develop properly, high fever, the presence of fibroid tumors in the uterus or an oddly formed uterus, both of which would mean too little space for the pregnancy to develop. Later miscarriages can happen because of placental insufficiency which failed to function adequately in servicing the baby, or because of a weak cervix which begins to dilate long before it should.

Occasionally there are underlying spiritual causes.

It sometimes happens that women who have had several abortions earlier in life have trouble carrying a child later; the body has received a repeated message, "abort," and now it obeys spontaneously. In such a case, forgiveness and healing are needed.

We have ministered to a number of women who were so wounded as children that they hated being children. Consciously or unconsciously, from a base of fear and anger, they vowed never to bring a child into such a troubled and hateful world. Now, as adults, they may consciously want to have children, but their inner computer is programed not to produce or sustain life. Either they have difficulty conceiving, or they miscarry repeatedly for no identifiable physical reasons.

If you are such a person, you need to *do* some forgiving of those who abused you. Fear, still alive in you at deep levels, needs to be ministered to by repeated prayers (preferably by someone else) for comfort, love, inner strength, and protection. God hears us the first time we pray. But our own inner being, like a little child, needs to hear messages of affirmation again and again before we can come to rest and trust. Following that, any possible inner vows not to produce life should be broken in prayer by someone who understands authority in the name of Jesus. By the same authority, the body should be directed to produce life and sustain it, according to God's original plan.

If you have experienced the disappointment of many miscarriages, you may have learned to perceive each regular menstrual period as the loss of a baby and an occasion to grieve. If that is the case, you then need to discipline yourself to choose life and face forward, regardless of your emotions, to take hold of the healing ministered to you by others.

According to the Bible there are also prevailing sinful conditions in our culture which contribute to an increasing incidence of miscarriage.

Chapter nine of Hosea speaks concerning the grossness of the nation's iniquity, their deep depravity, their coming to Baal-peor and devoting themselves to shame. Verse 11 says, ". . . their glory will fly away like a bird — no birth, no pregnancy and no conception!" Verse 14 says, "Give them a miscarrying womb and dry breasts."

In the last two years we have heard reports of an alarming increase in incidents of miscarriage in a number of places where we have traveled to teach. This is also a time in history when belief in the absoluteness of the laws of God has been eroded even from the hearts of many Christians. Sin is taken lightly.

Too many run into the house of God to sing His praises, and then run out to fornicate and commit adultery the rest of the week with little or no conscience. Sex is no longer held to be sacred by many in our modern culture. A man who knows "how to possess his own vessel in sanctification and honor, not in lustful passion" (I Thess. 4:4), is rare. Hosea's words apply to us today as well as to the nation of Israel more than 2700 years ago.

THIS DOES NOT NECESSARILY MEAN THAT THOSE WHO ARE EXPERIENCING MISCARRIAGES TODAY ARE REAPING FOR THEIR OWN INDIVIDUAL SIN. WE ARE A CORPORATE BODY. WE ALL REAP BLESSINGS FROM THE LABORS OF PEOPLE ALL OVER THE WORLD. WE ALSO REAP FOR THE SINS OF MANKIND. "He causes His sun to rise on the evil and the good, and sends rain on the righteous and the unrighteous"   (Matt. 5:45).

We all need to repent for the sexual sins of our culture, as well as our own individual transgressions, and pray earnestly for the protection and blessing of our children.

If you have experienced a miscarriage, allow yourself to grieve for your lost baby.

Don't try to comfort yourself by rationalizing, "Well, it doesn't matter; it didn't really have a chance to become a person. It's not really the same as losing a baby." Your baby was a person from the moment of conception. Even if you never felt your child move in your womb, the loss can be emotionally shattering.

Allow your feelings to live. Share them with your husband. If he hasn't yet really experienced the reality of the pregnancy, he may not have the same feelings of loss you do. If he seems detached, it doesn't mean he doesn't care. It doesn't necessarily mean he never really wanted a baby. Ask him to listen, and comfort you anyway. If he can't do that, talk with a woman friend who has gone through the same experience.

Cry your tears. Release to the Lord the little person you have lost, with your blessing, and look forward to a happier day when a healthy conception will be brought to full term. Relax. If you work too hard at trying to make that day happen, you'll ruin the spontaneity and blessedness of sexual union with your husband, and your increasing tension will decrease your chances of becoming pregnant again.

God sometimes graces the sorrowful with comforting assurances beyond their faith.

A friend of mine recently shared a beautiful testimony with me. She had gone through a series of deeply emotional, disturbing experiences which included many personal struggles with persecution and rejection, the death of a family member, and then finally a miscarriage which was devastating to her hopes and dreams. All of these hit her in the same period of time.

Though she was a new Christian, her relationship with the Lord was vital. She worked through forgiveness and the pain of grief and loss as well as she was able to do. But she continued to be troubled and oppressed by guilt feelings that she had never been able to give her lost baby anything but sorrow and death. She struggled with her feelings for nearly four years, impatient with her inability to let go and come to rest.

Then one day as she and her pastor were praying about the matter, he asked her what she would say to her baby if she could. "Go on, put your feelings into words; as if your baby were right here, tell her how you feel about her, what you wish you could have done together." She did just that, and as they resumed their prayers, God gave her a clear vision of her little girl's face in heaven, and opened her ears to hear her child's laughter. Not only that, but she heard peals of laughter from many children. At that moment she was able to let go of the grief she had carried for so long, knowing now, by the Lord's confirming gift, that her child had received life and happiness, not death.

God does not call us to build theologies on such testimonies. Neither does He call us to try to reproduce the same as a comforting technique. God will bring His gifts of comfort and healing to each one in the particular ways and times He chooses.

Working through the sufferings of stillbirth.

No amount of loving and sympathetic care and comfort can completely take away the suffering you experience when your child is stillborn, even though Jesus surely bears your griefs and carries your sorrows (Isa. 53:4), and friends and family want to give you support and comfort. You are not alone in your pain and grief, and your nagging guilt and fear, though you may experience excruciating loneliness.

People who are close to you reach out to help, not knowing what you are ready to hear or receive. Some have the wisdom to wait silently, loving you, empathetically burden-bearing with you, listening when you want to talk. Others, like Job's comforters, may offer absurdly inappropriate-at this-time advice to "put it behind you — cheer up, you can have another baby — don't cry, your baby is better off in heaven." Or they may insensitively pile impossible-to-handle-at-this-time emotional burdens on you with admonitions to take thought for your husband, or concentrate on the needs of your other children. Sometimes those on the hospital staff are gifted with godly wisdom, love and sensitivity. Sometimes they are not. Many will avoid mentioning the subject because they are having trouble handling their own feelings of helplessness to save your baby.

Whatever the reactions and capabilities of people around you, your own grieving is a very personal and intimate matter which only the Lord can understand — and at first you may not be able to receive what even He has to give. You may be too numb with shock to feel God's presence, or to be open to receive help with any comforting awareness of the presence of the flesh-and-blood people who are attending you. You may be struggling with anger — most often projected upon the medical staff who failed to warn or prepare you. Perhaps you can't shake the feeling that some tremendous error may have been committed.

You keep thinking, "Why me?" "Why, God, did you let this happen to *me*?" "It's not fair! People who don't even want babies have them. Lots of people abuse them and some even abandon or kill them! I just want a baby to love!" Sometimes when people come near to help, everything in you screams to be left alone. And sometimes when you *are* left alone, you feel abandoned.

There are no easy solutions. The grieving process can't be hurried or avoided. If you delay the process by denial or suppression or over-compensation (by hyper-faith or strength of will), you may be overwhelmed by grief or the stressful effects of ungrieved grief later.

Give yourself permission to grieve. If you are an emotional mess for a time, that does not mean you are weak. If you allow yourself to grieve, you will come out of the mess much faster.

If your husband is able to weep with you, hold you and communicate that the two of you can and will work it out together, that is wonderful! I remember the manly grief of my brother Jerry when he and his wife lost their first baby. But many men have been falsely taught by our culture that strong men don't cry. So their practiced response to emotional pain may be to exercise self-control and appear to be matter-of-fact, or to suppress and withdraw, or to get very busy with busy-nesses they can manage so as to feel competent.

They may even believe that what they are doing is necessary to support you or to be strong for the sake of the rest of the family. Some may find some inanimate thing to punch in order to relieve stress, or explode spontaneously on any person who happens to be in the vicinity. If your husband's reaction is in any way inappropriate to your feelings or your need, do not assume that he is not as pained as you. As isolated and rejected as you may feel, refuse to accept and feed your nagging thoughts that perhaps he does not love you, or that he *means* to abandon you when you need him the most.

If you become very depressed following the loss of your baby, understand that your body has poured tremendous energy into the nurturing of that little one for the full term of your pregnancy. Your excitement has mounted with anticipation of fulfillment of beautiful hopes and dreams. Now there is no baby to nurture, and your system snaps like an overstretched rubber band. But unlike the rubber band, when you have rested, and grieved your grief, you *will* rise again and regain resilience.

If you experience sexual problems for a while, don't worry about yourself or doubt your love for your husband. It is very difficult to experience sexual stimulation or pleasure when you are feeling depressed. Don't worry about yourself if you do begin to experience some pleasure and then feel a rush of tears. Know that this is a normal part of the process of coming back up again.

If you find yourself struggling with dreams about giving birth to a stillborn or damaged child, don't jump to interpret such a dream as a prophetic warning. It is probably no more than undealt-with wounds, fears and/or guilts expressing from your unconscious. Never suppress fears. Let them surface where they can be faced and overcome. Seek ministry from your pastor, counselor, or friend who can talk and pray with you about such things.

If you desperately want another baby, but can't shake your fears about possibly losing another, talk honestly with your doctor about your feelings. Let him comfort you by preparing your mind and heart with *facts*. Don't expect your doctor to be a spiritual or emotional *counselor* to you. Few are either trained or gifted to counsel. Most do not have time for counseling. But they can certainly disarm the anxieties that misinformation causes.

Some close friends of ours lost a grandchild several years ago. There had been no prior indication that there could be a serious problem. The entire family was emotionally devastated when their little boy was born with an undeveloped brain and with other parts missing or malformed. The baby only lived for a few hours. But during that time the family gave him all they could. His parents loved him. His grandparents held him in the nursery, rocked him and sang to him. They told him about Jesus.

His uncle talked to him and told him stories about the history of their family. Questions that anyone might have had about the baby's ability to understand were irrelevant. The family was pouring love into the personal spirit of a baby who needed to be claimed and treasured. And when he died, they blessed him and released him to his heavenly Father. Two years later the mother gave birth to a beautiful, healthy baby girl.

Sometimes a mother who has lost a baby, and then conceives another, tries to comfort herself with the thought that she is pregnant again with the child she lost. This can happen when the grieving process has not been completed, and emotional release and healing has not been accomplished. God doesn't recycle babies, and if that attitude and expectation prevails, the new baby may always struggle with a deep sense that he/she is a substitute for someone else. Such children may always feel they can't be loved for themselves.

Every baby is a unique person. Our friend's baby girl is not in any way a replacement for her brother who died. My brother Jerry and his wife were blessed with three fine sons after the loss of their first. but not one is a replacement for the first-born. Not one is like the others. Each is loved and appreciated as a unique gift of God.

What, then, fills the special empty place in the heart of the parents for the one they lost? Nothing but the countless expressions of the love of God over a period of time, and the believed promise of eternal life and reunion with our loved ones.

The Trauma of Losing an Older Child

The death of an older child is more difficult to deal with because you have had time to bond more securely. You and your husband have invested years of yourselves, shared countless, precious, tender moments with your children. You have played and worked and laughed and cried together. You have nursed them through the pain of scraped knees and hurt feelings again and again. You have comforted failures and celebrated achievements.

Many important family decisions have been made with top priority given to their well-being. You have been growing in excitement and expectancy concerning each child's capabilities and potential. You have the sense that if your children can become all that they can be, you live! It is not that you live *through* your children's life. But somehow your innermost being is set free to dance and sing and celebrate in a special, glorious way when you see you sons and daughters flourishing. You rejoice for their sake, and for the lives they will touch. Each child's roots are entwined deeply around your heart in such a way that when death uproots him/her, great violence is done to you.

Understanding and Dealing with Your Husband's Response

I mentioned earlier that often husbands cannot truly mourn a miscarriage because the conception has not yet become real to them. They have known you were pregnant, but they have not yet seen or touched or felt the presence of the child as you have. They have related more to an idea, a hope, a dream which can be replaced. A husband may express disappointment, and, if he is sensitive, he may sympathize or even empathize with his wife.

But he can't be expected to feel the loss of one he has never seen or held in the same degree you do. The same man can feel real grief (whether he can express it or not) for the loss of a stillborn baby, especially if he has been participating with his wife in the joy and wonder of the development process — listening to the heartbeat, placing his hand on her abdomen and blessing the little one in the womb. But he has not yet had the opportunity to bond with the baby in the same degree his wife has.

When an older child dies, your husband goes through the same deep emotional wrenching that you as a mother experience. He too has had time to bond, and feels that a part of himself has been ripped away. He is plagued with feelings of frustration and guilt, as you are, that you were helpless; you couldn't save your loved one from the illness or accident that took his/her life. You are hit again and again with a Niagara of thoughts about what you wish you had said to your child or done for him while he was alive.

If the two of you can share your grief together, console one another, and pray for one another, your relationship will naturally grow stronger. But if either of you is paralyzed by an inability to express emotions or share pain, and withdraws into isolation, the other is left to struggle with overwhelming feelings of rejection and abandonment. A chasm can grow between you that becomes more and more difficult to span.

As I have said before, men in our culture have been more disequipped than women in the area of free and healthy expression of emotion. Your husband is the one most likely to withdraw. Understand what is really happening. Do not allow yourself to perceive his closedness as personal rejection and abandonment. Insofar as you are able, with God helping you:

Do not react in kind. Two people withdrawing only widen the chasm.
 Do not accuse or manipulate.
  For your own sake find a "safe" friend or
   counselor (you are vulnerable) with whom to
talk and pray.

Pray for your husband to have strength of spirit to
 let his emotions live,
  to open his heart and let you in,
   to talk with you.

Pray that the Lord will supply your need, and bring
 every message of demand in you to death.

Touch your husband with gentle, sensitive affection
as often as he
  will allow. If he pushes you away, understand that
   he does so out of fear of losing control. Back
    off, pray silently for him, and try again later.
     Pray that your touch will be comfort,
      blessing, and *invitation*.

When tempted to say to him, "Don't you know . . .?"
— "Can't you see . . .?" — "Why can't you . . .?" — zip
your lip, and say something more along the lines of,
"You're hurting, aren't you? I understand." Sensitive,

loving, affirmative persistence is a powerfully effective (though not guaranteed) bridge to span chasms created by grief, hurt and fear.

The kind of discipline I have described is not easy when your own heart is bleeding. You can't keep from feeling that your husband is supposed to be the priest of the house. He should be concerned for you, and taking some kind of initiative toward you. It doesn't seem fair. Why should you have to be the "strong" one?

It is natural for you to feel as you do, but if you hold on to those feelings and feed them or wallow in them, you may fall into dark depths of depression that fill the chasm between you. It is far more difficult to rise from that. God will empower your attempts to forgive, heal, bless, and confront in love. He will not empower your choices to hold on to anger, bitterness, self-pity or accusation, or to wield them as weapons of aggression or defense.

Understanding Your Own Responses

Suppose you find yourself crying incessantly and uncontrollably in the grieving process. You can't understand what is the matter with you. You are trying to relate to your husband in a sensitive and loving way, but it seems impossible when you are a total mess of emotions. The more emotional you become, the farther he flees from you. You feel strange, alien even to yourself, and you begin to fear that you could be headed toward a nervous breakdown.

There are at least two powerful dynamics at work here. In chapter two I spoke of the way in which a wife unconsciously identifies with her husband because of their one-flesh relationship. She experiences the feelings he cannot express, carries the burdens he has not talked about, and cries the tears he cannot cry. When parents have lost a child, and the father withdraws into isolation, tightly bound by intense, ungrieved grief, and fears sharing with anyone, his wife may carry the load and cry for both of them.

The second dynamic in operation is what my husband, John, and I call the "balance principle." If one partner is extremely talkative, the other becomes quiet. If one fails to discipline the children, the other tends to over-discipline. If one seems foolishly adventurous, the other develops a cautious attitude that appears to be cowardice.

We were created to complement, uplift and strengthen one another in our differentnesses. But when significant areas of our personality have not yet been surrendered to God, and redeemed, we are too much controlled by old habitual practices in our nature. Then instead of blessing and fulfilling each other, we drive one another to extremes.

If a husband cannot express his hurt and grief openly, his wife will probably go to the other extreme with the combined weight and power of the grief in both of them. She can't understand why she has become so emotional and nearly out of control, but it is only that she is counterbalancing her husband and bearing his ungrieved grief.

If this is what is happening to you, what can you do? Recognize the dynamics at work. Quit worrying about your sanity. Tell the Lord about it. Lift and relinquish *all* the load to Him. And go about your business. Repeat. Repeat. Repeat. . . until it is no longer a problem.

There are consecutive stages of grief connected with any loss: denial, anger and guilt, depression, acceptance, and then healing. We need to know that God loves us as we move through that natural sequence in the gift of His grace.

Where Is the Final Consolation in Relation to a Child Who Dies?
His life and legacy

My little cousin Charlie was one of God's special gifts. He was a beautiful boy with an outstanding, keen intellect, a bright, happy nature, and a zest for living that inspired all the family. I remember vividly his soft, blond, curly hair and blue eyes, delightfully entertaining chatter, sense of humor, and enthusiastic hugs.

He loved the stories the family read to him, and had memorized most of them word for word. He loved to sing, and could carry a tune very well. His favorite songs were the ones he learned at Sunday school. When he sang "Jesus loves me, this I know," we knew he knew from the depths of his heart the truth of what what he was singing.

Before Charlie started kindergarten he went into the hospital for what everyone thought would be a simple tonsillectomy. Something went wrong. We never knew just what it was. Someone guessed it might have been an allergy to the anesthetic.

Little Charlie died. But before he died he left a beautiful gift for us to remember — a gift which exemplified the blessing his short life had been. His parents went in to see him as he was coming out of the anesthetic, and he said to them, "I'm so sorry I can't sing for you today."

His Inheritance

There is a story in the Bible which says it all:

And they were bringing children to Him so that He might touch them; and the disciples rebuked them. But when Jesus saw this, He was indignant and said to them, *'Permit the children to come to Me; do not hinder them; for the kingdom of God belongs to such as these.* Truly I say to you, whoever does not receive the kingdom of God like a child shall not enter it at all.' *And He took them in His arms and began blessing them, laying His hands upon them.*   (Mark 10:13-16)

From the Guilt of Abortion — to Forgiveness to Freedom to Blessing

We live in a crazy, mixed-up, sinful world where thousands of people who can't even feed themselves give birth to babies who suffer from malnutrition and eventually die as helpless mothers' hearts are broken. More tragic than that is the murdering of millions of babies in wombs of mothers who *could* provide for their offspring, but choose not to. Some act in fear and panic, unable to believe they have any alternative, and may grieve deeply.

Others dehumanize the children they have killed for convenience sake, in order to rationalize their actions and deny their guilt. What they don't realize is that while "fetus" may *sound* more like a "thing" than a "person," it is really only the Latin word for "baby." Though many women feel relieved initially after an abortion, suppressed guilt and ungrieved grief eventually take a tremendous toll in illness or nervous disorders, and they find themselves in desperate need of healing.

Healing is available for these women. Receiving forgiveness is a natural consequence of repentance for sin. And forgiveness lays the groundwork for healing that God *longs* to bring. But repentance is the key. Repentance for:

giving in to someone's pressure to get rid of an unwanted child — accepting the lie that it was okay, that you were justified by your unique circumstances — not wanting to be bothered — choosing material comforts rather than the life of the baby, your own flesh — being afraid of the responsibility of raising a child, or being too young — hiding the embarrassment of illegitimacy —

whatever you thought your reasons were —
repentance for *murdering* your child.

It sounds so harsh to put it that way, but until you
repent of the abortion as a murder, you will never be
free. Guilt is your friend. You can't receive forgiveness
until you admit your guilt. Guilt is not the same thing
as condemnation. Murder is not the unforgiveable sin.
Rationalization will hold you forever in bondage to the
stresses of hidden guilt and the compulsive need for
self-defense. To know you are forgiven is to be truly
free to get on with your life.

Many women have come to John and me, weighted
down because of a past abortion. Normally we don't
push people to have an emotional experience. But in
the case of abortion, we know that since they had to
"dehumanize" their baby in some way in order to kill
it — i.e. by calling it "fetus" or a "product of conception"
— since they have lived for a long time in that practice
of denying reality, they need now to give themselves
permission to experience some real emotions about the
death of their child. We suggest:

Ask yourself (or ask God to let you know) if the baby
would have been a boy or a girl.

What might you have named the baby?

What might this child have looked like?

What might the child have accomplished in his/her
life?

As women have pondered these questions, some have
discovered surprising and heart-wrenching reality in
dreams, in visions, or in "just knowing." And almost

all have broken through to sob and sob in grief for their lost child. "For the sorrow that is according to the will of God produces a repentance without regret, leading to salvation; but the sorrow of the world produces death" (2 Cor. 7:10). With the deep sobbing has come cleansing and healing and with forgiveness, the beginning of restored health and self-esteem.

Children Are Gifts Sent From God, not Ordered From Convenience Stores.

Though most of our children came as surprises, and none of them at "convenient" times, I fought with everything within me not to lose them. The cold, hard logic of the world would have said we couldn't afford them, but somehow overwhelming love rose up from within John and me to welcome and embrace each one. By God's grace we've managed to get through college and seminary, feed and clothe and educate the kids, pay our bills, and enjoy a rich, stimulating, challenging, fulfilling and fun-filled family life and ministry all along the way. Praise God for the quiver full of arrows He gave us!

6
Living With Too Many Signals

I just gave my computer too many signals at the same time, and it had the good sense not to try to respond to them all at once. It simply refused to do anything until I turned it off for a moment and started it again with one signal at a time. I have often wished the computers of our inner being were as quick to stop in response to overload, and as obedient to proper new directions following a time of rest and reflection.

If we persist in overloading our mental, emotional or spiritual circuits without taking sufficient time to sort out, prioritize, digest and pray, we run into confusion. And then if we plunge ahead to press the "print" button, the garbled messages we project fail miserably to communicate in a redemptive way what is in our hearts.

John and I used to have a very large garden. The biggest and most beautiful vegetables in the neighborhood came from that 100'-by-35' piece of fertile ground. Visitors regularly stopped to admire, and more than a few pronounced their blessings. I was truly grateful for the unbelievable abundance of produce from the garden and I thought I was well prepared for hours of canning and freezing. But when John's mounting excitement inspired him to keep bringing in huge heaps of harvest onto my kitchen counters and table, my gratitude diminished rather quickly. Instead of being able to picture rows on rows of colorful jars filled with bountiful store for winter, I felt like I was suffocating under an increasing mountain of carrots and tomatoes and corn and beans! I had no space to work, and the task viewed all at once was too much!

My first objections carried emotional overtones that seemed to John to communicate a lack of appreciation, and resistance to putting forth the efforts necessary to preserve the precious treasures of his garden. I don't remember what he said, but I was convinced he didn't understand at all where I was coming from. We could have become lost in a mess of feelings, far afoul of truth, if we had not stopped to pray, sort it out logically together, and choose to hear and embrace with respect what the other was feeling.

John was finally persuaded to deposit on the porch all but what I considered to be a reasonable amount to handle at once. And I proceeded joyfully to accomplish the project one step at a time — with some very willing help from him.

Several years ago someone spoke to me following a conference in Cincinnati, Ohio, where John and I had taught what we considered to be simple basics of biblical counseling.

"This was absolutely wonderful! Beyond my expectations! But it's the first time I've been fed with a fire hose!"

"How does it make you feel?" I asked. "Like you need to burp?"

"I don't really know. I guess I'm afraid I won't be able to remember it all."

"Don't try. Go home and do something absolutely earthy, something fun and relaxing. Everything will fall into place, and you'll find yourself remembering when you need it. No cause for sweat. If it's important, God will bring it up and run it by again."

"Okay!"

The word I gave to that person was received as welcome relief. The admonition to relax and let everything settle met no resistance because their anxiety feelings had only been in reaction to too many positive signals. But when negative signals have come with the force of a fire hose, the recipient finds it extremely difficult to embrace any kind of a "let it go for now" message. Letting go sounds like an invitation to irresponsibility or insanity and destruction.

Concerning the Nature and Place of Feelings

For most people, feelings often falsely represent objective reality. They don't understand that *our personal feelings have to do only with our subjective experiences, interpretations, and responses,* and that our experiences are limited, our interpretations are colored, and our responses are greatly influenced by what has lodged in our hearts already — from an accumulation of current unhealed, unreleased stresses, or perhaps even from earliest childhood experiences. Feelings are affected by what we have eaten, how well we have slept, what time of the month it is, whether the man in our life has recently and sincerely kissed us, how many times the phone has rung while we have been trying to prepare dinner, etc.

Telling people, especially women, who have come under a tyranny of negative feelings, to focus on something else for a little while, until their emotions settle, so that time and distance can grant a more balanced perspective, is liable to be received by them as rejection. You "don't understand the problem." You "don't accept" them. You have "questioned the validity" of their perceptions. You "don't respect" the way they feel, and they are hurt.

Because they have exalted their personal feelings as *truth,* they defend and nurse their feelings, and therefore are easily taken captive by them. When someone suggests a need to relax, that a situation might not warrant such intensity, these people often feel accused. "You don't think I ought to feel upset?!" "Wouldn't you be upset if that had happened to you?" "You're saying there is something wrong with me!"

They then have only two alternatives: they can hide or deny their feelings, plus suppress them and wallow in them, or, they can exalt their feelings, insist, persist — and wallow! They usually do the latter. But even if they choose denial, it is only a matter of time before the pressure of what has been suppressed increases to the point of an eruption. The wallowing time is what has increased the force of the explosion, whereas had they not believed and nurtured their feelings, time would have brought balance and rest.

Few who exalt their feelings can successfully shut them down, but those who are successful in turning off their emotions most often also lose the capacity to feel the positive emotions that enable one to experience zest for life. One can spiral into depression from either direction.

Everyone Has Feelings. The Important Thing Is What We Learn to Do With Them.

We should allow our feelings to live. Even though they often fail to represent objective truth, they are good indicators of what has lodged in our hearts. But we are in trouble if our minds make decisions solely on the basis of what we are feeling. Our hearts' emotions were not intended to rule our minds and direct our actions.

> For from *within,* out of the *heart* of men, proceed the evil thoughts, fornications, thefts, murders, adulteries, deeds of coveting and wickedness, as well as deceit, sensuality, envy, slander, pride and foolishness. All these evil things proceed from *within* and defile the man.   (Mark 7:21-23)

Rather, we are to be *renewed* in the spirit of our *minds* (Eph. 4:23), so that with the renewed mind we may instruct our heart in what to do with the emotions we feel, how to act, and how to "put on the new self, created to be like God in *true* righteousness and holiness" (Eph. 4:24, NIV)

John and I had taught these principles for years, thinking we understood what we were saying. But what we had known with our minds is now much better known with our hearts.

There Are Seasons When Floods Rise and Torrents Which Test Our Foundations Burst Against Our House. (Luke 6:48)

Several years ago John and I came home hoping to find rest from an intense traveling and teaching schedule, only to be hit with a series of the most stressful and emotionally disturbing situations we have ever had to face. First, we discovered that one of our sons-in-law had been molesting our granddaughter. She had fled into a classic running pattern which made it nearly impossible to reach her at the time. Not only had the ability to trust been fractured in her, but our daughter's ability to trust her husband was shattered.

Our daughter had been standing staunchly, consistently striving to forgive a husband who had kept on violating her ability to trust repeatedly in other areas. Now, she found herself fighting to control her emotions as she alternated between responding on the one hand like a bewildered, wounded lamb and on the other as a fierce mama bear. At last she knew she had to divorce her husband and spend herself trying to hold her remaining family together.

One grandson was too young to understand all that was going on; he simply ached, and wept for his father. The other grandson understood beyond his years, and could not be prevented from taking too much emotional responsibility for his family. He was a diabetic and the stress threw his insulin out of balance; he spent several weeks in the hospital in the intensive care unit.

John and I discovered we were capable of powerful feelings we had never known before. We had always been able to identify empathetically with counselees in the counseling process. But it was somewhat devastating and certainly humbling to realize that we could hate as deeply as we loved, and that we could even want to kill!

It took an unbelievable amount of grace and discipline in prayer, as well as every ounce of energy we had, to make the requisite choices to forgive (Matt. 6:14,15), not just once but again and again over an extended period of time as things got worse and worse. It stretched our faith tremendously to continue to make ourselves believe that the Lord could bring good out of such a mess as this. Though His work is not yet completed, He has, and is, faithfully, bit by bit, turning ashes into garlands in the life of each one involved. We are tremendously thankful.

While this was going on, a highly placed employee who was a very close friend at the time betrayed us and the ministry by gross unrepented sins in his own life. We had to dismiss him. A few in the local community, not understanding the circumstances, turned against us for that. We struggled with more feelings, and had to make aggressive choices to forgive.

At the same time, the man who was then our publisher — *not Victory House, the present one* — defaulted on payment of book royalties to us and many other authors. The publisher's accountant declared that $31,000 was owed to us, but the owner denied it! We found another publisher. More feelings. More choices. More hours of prayer on bended knees.

All of this happened during the same months in which a book became extremely popular in which the author attacked almost every ministry having anything to do with healing. His scholarship was atrocious! We and others were grossly misrepresented and misquoted. Disappointingly, far too many readers did not possess sufficient information to challenge his errors, or discernment to see what was happening. The Christian book market in general suffered.

Our books, among those more directly and falsely attacked, fell from being best-sellers to one-third of former sales for a time. But the feelings with which we had to struggle the most were hurts and griefs for the many people who had now become afraid to reach out for help anywhere for fear of getting into something they had been led to believe might be erroneous or even occultic.

We were disillusioned to find again and again that most of the Christians who objected to ours and others' teachings were reacting on the basis of hearsay — they had never even read or heard first-hand the material they were reviling and rejecting! We grieved also because of the division aggravated in the Body of Christ.

Where Was God?

Admittedly, like the Psalmists, we wondered from time to time where the Lord was while all this was going on. We had been walking His walk as best we knew how. We had no lack of testimonies concerning miracles of healing the Lord had accomplished throughout our ministry. Was He tending His flock? Though mentally we knew the answer very well, we found ourselves straining at emotional levels.

He reminded us that He hadn't promised to keep us out of all difficulty, and that He could take care of His wounded children and torn body. Scripture says there will be various trials. What God did promise was that He would be with us *in* trouble (Ps. 91:15). In our listening during our devotional times, the Lord also said to us that because of free will, He cannot and will not prevent anyone from sinning. But He will hold each accountable.

So we spent a lot of time in prayer,
    acknowledging our feelings each time they appeared,
    giving them to the Lord, raw and unpolished
(He is big enough to hear honest confessions without falling off His throne).

We kept asking His forgiveness for our anger and
resentment,
   telling Him we didn't know how to accomplish
   forgiveness toward others,
      but we were willing to make the choices
      anyhow,
      and would trust Him to make our choices real.

Obediently, we prayed blessing for our enemies.
God has been faithful. He is blessing us beyond our
expectations. Satan has not stolen our joy in the Lord,
nor has He prevented Jesus' redemptive process. Our
blood pressure has remained normal, and we have no
ulcers.

**Everyone has feelings, but men and women
handle them differently.**

During this stressful time I learned something about
the difference between men's and women's emotions.
I had always wondered why so many men seem to be
detached emotionally in crisis times. Sometimes I would
hurt so badly I could almost hear my insides screaming.
And as I prayed in intercession, I would occasionally
feel physical pain, as if I were in the last stages of
childbirth. But even giving birth to six children had
held far less cumulative pain than what we were
presently enduring.

Each time another detail of the one-after-another
blows would hit, I would feel a new wave of pain and
nausea, and weep, at least on the inside. John seemed

most often to stiffen up and withdraw. He sometimes appeared on the surface to be hard and uncaring. But I knew he was every bit as sensitive and caring as I.

Nevertheless, while I wanted him to be as solid *as* a rock, I didn't want him to *be* one. I wanted him to cry with me, but he couldn't or wouldn't. I couldn't understand why. When I tried to talk to him concerning my feelings, my efforts seemed only to drive him more deeply behind the walls of his private retreat, or into the oblivion of the television.

"John, I'm sorry I don't have a 'right' way to express myself. I'm just hurting. I can't 'find' you, and we need to stand together."

Silence.

"John, where are you? What are you doing in there all by yourself?"

"I'm just thinking."

"What are you thinking?"

"I don't know. I'm not ready to talk about it yet."

"I wish you could present your thoughts unpolished. Share the process with me."

Silence.

I knew that to press John further would be like beating on a deep bruise. So I described my feelings to the Lord, and understood that I could not expect John, who was every bit as wounded as I, to do for me what only God could do. I prayed comfort and strength of spirit for my husband and saturated myself

with the Word of God which is infinitely substantial
and true:

> I sought the LORD, and He answered me, and
> delivered me from all my fears.   (Ps. 34:4)

> Do not fret because of evildoers... for they will
> wither quickly like the grass... Trust in the LORD
> and do good ... and He will give you the desires
> of your heart. Commit your way to the LORD,
> trust also in Him———and He will bring forth our
> righteousness as the light, and your judgment as
> the noonday. Rest in the LORD and wait patiently
> for Him; do not fret because of him who prospers
> in his way... Cease from anger, and forsake
> wrath...   (Ps. 37:1-8)

I talked to myself:

> Why are you in despair, O my soul? And why have
> you become disturbed within me? *Hope in God, for
> I shall again praise Him for the help of His presence.*
>   (Ps. 42:5)

At first I was just going through the motions —
choosing and persisting in a discipline because I knew
I had to. In the process God made His presence real
to me. I know that John, in his way, was doing likewise.

Our daughter, in the intensity and confusion of her
shattered life, had to do the same thing. She was able
to share some feelings with loved ones who listened
and supported and prayed for her. But no one but God
could reach the innermost core of the terrible hurt, pain,

insecurity, loneliness and anxiety which threatened for a while to drag her into craziness.

Despite her feelings, she struggled to persist in a discipline of choosing to do what she knew would put her in a place of receiving from the Lord. Even while inner emotional foundations seemed to be slipping, and her world was falling down around her, she continued to attend church and her kinship group, to teach her Sunday school class, to read the Word, pray, and choose to peg her life on what she wasn't able at that time to experience. In the process, Father God showed up with gifts of strength to stand, grace to forgive, loving kindness to enable repentance, and real redemptive power.

The question remained: Why could Ami and I verbalize feelings so much more easily than John? Why does this difference between men and women manifest so consistently to cause hurtful misunderstandings and frustration?

Learning to Understand and Appreciate My "Brain-Damaged" Husband.

We found some answers when we listened to a tape of an enlightening interview by James Dobson with Dr. Donald Joy who reported concerning some research being done on the right and left brain in males and females. We were somewhat amused at first, but all kinds of lights began to turn on. The following is from an article written by Gary Smalley and John Trent on that very subject.

Medical studies have shown that between the 18th and 26th weeks of pregnancy, something happens that forever separates the sexes. Using heat-sensitive monitors, researchers have actually observed a chemical bath of testosterone and other sex-related hormones wash over a baby boy's brain. This causes changes that never happen to a baby girl. Here's a layman's explanation of what happens when those chemicals hit a boy's system.

The human brain is divided into two halves, or hemispheres, connected by fibrous tissue called the corpus callosum. The sex-related hormones that flood a baby boy's brain cause the right side to recede slightly, destroying some of the connecting fibers. One result is that, in most cases, a boy starts life more left-brain oriented.

Because little girls don't experience this chemical bath, they leave the starting blocks much more two-sided in their thinking. And while electrical impulses and messages do travel back and forth between both sides of a baby boy's brain, those same messages can proceed faster and be less hindered in the brain of a little girl.

Now wait a minute, you may be thinking. Does this mean that men are basically brain-damaged?

Well, not exactly. What occurs in the womb merely sets the stage for men and women to 'specialize' in two different ways of thinking. And this is one major reason men and women need each other so much.

The left brain houses more of the logical, analytical, factual, and aggressive centers of thought. It's the side of the brain most men reserve for most of their waking hours. It enjoys conquering 500 miles a day on family vacation trips; favors mathematical formulas over romance novels; stores the dictionary definition of love; and generally favors clinical, black-and-white thinking.

On the other hand, most women spend the majority of their days and nights camped out on the right side of the brain. It's the side that harbors the center for feelings, as well as the primary relational, language and communication skills; enables them to do fine detail work; sparks imagination; and makes an afternoon devoted to art and fine music actually enjoyable. Perhaps you can begin to understand why communication is difficult in marriage. . . .

Since men are primarily left-brain oriented, they generally focus on the words being said and often miss the underlying emotions. (Gary Smalley and John Trent, "Why Can't My Spouse Understand What I Say?," *Focus on the Family,* November, 1988, p.3.)

We women can feel so alone when that important underlying part of us is missed!

I remember well the years when our six children were growing up, and I was a busy pastor's wife. The doorbell and the telephone were almost continually in competition with the children for my attention. I never knew when someone's crisis would arrive on our doorstep, or when our dinner would need to be stretched to feed someone who was hungry for food and/or tender loving care.

Our backyard was always full of the neighbors' children, to the extent that we laughingly (most of the time) threatened to put up a sign saying, "Public Playground — Everybody Welcome." I always had to be ready for a spontaneous invasion of little people who were forever needing to get a drink or use the potty. Teenagers from the church frequently dropped by after school and stayed to talk awhile.

Prayer meetings and youth group meetings were usually held in our home, largely because we couldn't afford to have a baby-sitter. Sunday looked nothing like a day of rest for us, and at that time we had not yet learned to say "no" to those who called on Monday to plead, "I know this is your day off, but I'm dying." "Free time" was not even a part of my vocabulary.

Sometimes John would come home, recognize a quality of frazzledness in my countenance, and say, "Honey, you look tired. Maybe we could go out to eat this evening." Being the practical and thrifty person that I am, I would respond, "That would be great, John, but we really can't afford it."

At that point, if he heard only the words I said, and replied, "You're right, we can't," and let it go at that, he would have been logically in line with the stated truth of our financial condition. But he would have missed the essential meaning of my message. I would then have struggled with vague, confused feelings of being misunderstood or baited and let down (rather like a pooped and panting puppy who ran but never caught the bone), and feelings of guilt for entertaining those emotions even as I meditated on the unfairness of that day's martyrdom.

What I was really saying was that I was glad he noticed how tired I was; that though I was aware of the limitations of our budget, I desperately hoped we would have more regard for me than the budget. (McDonald's would do!) I wanted him to press beyond my protest to persuade me to receive the blessing of his gift because he loved me.

Early in our marriage John asked me, "Why don't you just say what you mean?" I said to him, "Because you're supposed to know!" He was mystified. It was difficult to make him understand how my having to tell him what I wanted could spoil the blessing of his giving so as to make me feel unloved or unappreciated. I was supposed to know that he loved me whether he thought to tell me or not!

Each of us has had to recognize many habits of thinking and feeling in *"supposed to"* terms, to die to our demands, and believe that we are chosen and cherished by the other despite our differentnesses in perceptions and responses. I had to learn not to take personally his "hard" logic that occasionally seemed to disrespect and offend my sensitivities. Over the years I have grown to appreciate John's ability to help me sort and order my sometimes overwhelming flood of feelings with his peculiarly male thought patterns. And he has learned to receive with respect my perceptions which, though usually accurate, sometimes lack a conscious and explainable concrete premise.

Because I am a woman, I can simultaneously cook dinner, talk on the telephone, hug one child as he comes past me in the kitchen, and still be alertly aware of the baby who has just headed toward the open door to the stairway. My beloved, "brain-damaged" husband usually focuses on one thing at a time. It is in one sense a blessing that he can completely tune out noise and motion to read, pray, write and create with rapt concentration. But if I were not nearby to receive and attend to the multitude of signals he has tuned out, our family could possibly be in trouble.

I used to be quite perturbed with John when he would become so totally occupied with what he was doing that he failed to hear or see what our young children were doing. I thought he was being negligent because of a warped or underdeveloped sense of priority. When our oldest son, Loren, was a year old he lavishly decorated our entire living-room floor with talcum powder while his father sat in the same room, reading. Coming back into our apartment, I fairly shrieked, "John — how *could* you not see what he was doing!?" Now as grandparents we are older and wiser. When John watches the little grandchildren, that is what he does — he watches the grandchildren.

The Problem of Small Talk

Women often talk with one another about what everyone already knows, and if it doesn't go on endlessly, we will enjoy the conversation. Men can't understand that at all. They may even feel insulted if a woman persists in delivering to them information which, to their way of thinking, contains nothing new or edifying. It sounds to them like a waste of time. Or like endless repetition of stories bordering on gossip. They may say so, and seriously wound the sensitivities of women they care about.

Many men tend to be bored and impatient with embellishments that seem not to be central to issues. Most of the time they don't understand that women communicate far more than verbal messages when we talk. We may be only venting stress. But more often we are tuning in to one another beneath the messages, sharing nuances of feeling and forming emotional bridges and parameters for relationships.

Words spoken may merely be vehicles for what is actually being given or received from heart to heart and spirit to spirit. I am not at all sure that many women are consciously aware of this dynamic. We simply do what we do. But I am certain that women are often deeply wounded when men we care about seem to belittle or ridicule us — even when it is only by humorously or affectionately flavored comments. Understanding that men function in a different emotional way than females, and that many aspects of us are a mystery to them, should help us not to receive every negative-sounding comment as personal criticism and rejection.

As often as possible, John and I get together with our friends Ken and Donna to play pinochle. Donna and I can carry on an animated conversation while we play, and still do our share of winning. We can bound up to answer the phone and not be overly bothered or distracted.

But when Ken and John play cards, *they play cards!* Our conversation and telephone interruptions drive them crazy — especially when we talk and win! So we try (sometimes successfully) to confine our talk to interludes while new hands are being dealt. Men are made more for single-minded activity and they need us to understand and meet them where they are.

With the four of us, this is becoming a subject for good-natured joking and teasing. But unfortunately, with many couples, a situation such as I have just described becomes a very serious issue which kills their good time together and compounds other stressful issues between them.

Not only are Donna and I more easily able to respond to a multiplicity of stimuli; we are more spontaneous and emotional than Ken or John. This is not because of immaturity or a lack of self-discipline, but because we are made that way. We need our husbands to complete us, and on occasion to firmly and dispassionately settle us when our ability to receive and transmit multi-signals is over-taxed and our emotional wiring begins to short out. God has designed and equipped us all — not to battle — but to appreciate and bless and balance one another with our differentnesses. How do we do that?

There Is a Discipline to Walk in.
We Must:

Recognize our basic differences without putting any value judgment on them. God knew what He was doing when He made us the way He did.

Die to our demands that another person think and feel like we do. If men and women were alike, it might be comfortable, but would certainly be boring. And we would lose the value of the balance principle.

Choose to forgive when others treat us insensitively.

Isn't that what women want from men? Eventually we get what we give. (Matt. 6:14,15, Gal. 6:7, Matt. 7:1,2)

Know that we can't make forgiveness happen. That is God's task.

Our job is to make the choice, again and again. Unforgiveness held in the heart is a poison that will defile others and eventually destroy us. It is also a force which warps our perspective and prevents us from recognizing the other person's attempts to change for the better. And it is a seed sown which will cause us to reap in kind.

Tell God immediately how we feel about an injury or slight. Do this in a *flash prayer* before the emotion has a chance to lodge in our hearts. He is big enough to handle the full force of our initial uncensored, unsorted, unpolished emotions. Our spouses and children, friends and associates, probably are not.

You may protest, "But I'm not a Christian! I'm not even sure I believe God is real. Or — if He is — why should He listen to me?"

Try this consistently over a period of time anyway, and see what a difference it makes!

Ask God to speak His best response through us. This may be silence.

It may be a soft word. It may be a stern word.

It may be an apology, an explanation, or a confrontation. It may even be a choice to separate from him for a time.

The important thing is, if we submit our fleshly response to God without defending our self-righteousness, He then has an opportunity to express a redemptive word or deed through us which, by His Spirit, can possibly contribute to healing and reconciliation, and to the building of relationship.

Something deeper may be necessary.

If we continue to struggle unsuccessfully in the same areas, we would be wise to talk and pray with a counselor concerning the possible *root* causes for the fruit produced repeatedly in our lives:

For there is no good tree which produces bad fruit.
(Luke 6:43a).

We may have experienced wounds during our foundational years *(before we were six)* for which fear, resentment and bitterness have been stored in our hearts. These may hold us in bondage, shaping and fueling our present responses to hurt. They may perpetuate childish ways of thinking and feeling and doing, thus keeping us from making decisions we want to make, and acting on them.

George comes home tired and wanting quiet time to collect himself before dinner. He gives his wife, Mary, a quick "Hi, what's for supper?" before he sinks into his favorite chair and turns the TV on. Mary thinks to herself, "That's okay. A kiss would have been nice, but he's tired. He'll feel better after dinner." No problem. (So far.)

Dinner is ready. Mary issues a call to the children playing in the backyard and to her husband who is staring with rapt attention at the TV. Four enthusiastically hungry children come running through the back door; the littlest one falls down under the feet of the mob as they enter the kitchen.

Mary comforts wounded feelings and a bumped head and ushers the troops to the bathroom to wash. Four children rush to the table to sit down. One manages somehow to knock over his glass of milk as he takes his seat. Mary mops up the mess, and takes her place at the table. All is ready, and the children are waiting eagerly for the table grace to be said. The head of the household is missing, hypnotized by the action on the five-yard line.

"George, dinner is ready."

"Okay — just a minute."

"George, everyone is ready. Didn't you hear me call you?"

"No — but I'll be there in a minute. They're on the five-yard line."

"George, the children are hungry. We're all at the table and the food is getting cold. Will you *please* come — now!?"

George comes — by way of the bathroom. Minutes pass.

"George, are you coming!? Shall we go ahead without you!?

"Mary, get off my back! I'm tired and I don't need that yackety-yack."

George thinks he has sent one clear signal to Mary which she should understand and respect. He's tired, and he didn't hear her call, and he came as soon as he could. Mary, by this time, is being hit with all kinds of signals:

1. Does he think he's the only one who has worked all day? I'd like to get lost once in a while in the TV, but who'd watch the kids?

2. I called him in plenty of time. The kids heard me from the back yard. Is he deaf?

3. Why should I fix a good hot meal and let it sit there and get cold because he has to watch one more play? They'll re-run it on the late news anyway.

4. Doesn't he know what kind of example he's setting for his children?

5. Doesn't he know what that communicates to his kids? How important are they anyway? What happened to priorities?

6. Why did George have to snap at me like that in front of the children?

7. Why are men always so insensitive?

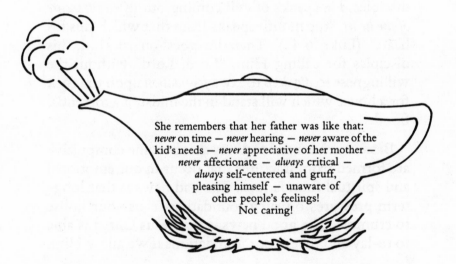

She remembers that her father was like that: *never* on time — *never* hearing — *never* aware of the kid's needs — *never* appreciative of her mother — *never* affectionate — *always* critical — *always* self-centered and gruff, pleasing himself — unaware of other people's feelings! Not caring!

Mary then directs an angry "Why do you *always*...why do you *never*...?" toward her husband with all the steam from an interior boiling pot of judgment, unforgiveness, and bitter-root expectancy lodged in her heart from her childhood. She is for the moment so overcome by her own feelings, she can't discern or control her over-reaction. And she won't be able to stop the steam until she deals with the fire under the pot.

Some Christians Today Think This Sounds Like Psychology.
Where Do We Find This Kind of Understanding in the Bible?
Did Jesus Ever Say Anything Like This?

The message in Luke 6 is spoken by Jesus to His disciples. He speaks of evil coming out of the *treasure of the heart,* "the mouth speaks from that which fills his heart" (Luke 6:45). Then he goes on to chide his disciples for calling Him, "Lord, Lord" without the willingness to *dig deep* to lay a *foundation* upon the rock for a house which will stand in the midst of a torrential flood.

Basic attitudes and feelings that become compulsive are formed from fractures that occur in our emotional and spiritual foundations. The bad news is that long-term pressures on such foundations cause our house to crumble. The good news is that Jesus Christ is able to re-lay and renew our foundations if we allow Him.

Colossians 3 and Ephesians 4 both refer to the tree of us and its fruit, calling it our "old self with its evil *practices*" (Col 3:9) which must be put away once we have come to Jesus. Habitual ways of thinking, feeling, reasoning, speaking, and acting are not easily changed. They are *"childish things"* (1 Cor. 13:11) that are done away with only as we mature and have new practices built in us.

Many Christians celebrate that they are new creatures and resist the idea that they now have anything within the heart to deal with. Yet they struggle and often fail to live the life and faith they profess. The Word of God is clear:

> Our old self was crucified with Him, *that our body of sin might be done away with,* that we should no longer be slaves to sin; for he who had died is freed from sin. (Rom. 6:6,7)

"Our body of sin" (not our sinful body) is made up not only of the recognizably sinful thoughts and deeds we have committed, but of *all* the old habits and practices we built before we became new creatures. We have not known ways other than those which we have already experienced. The new creature has to practice new motives and modes of operating. We are like babes who have just learned to crawl.

Crawling may sometimes be frustrating, hard on the knees, and dirt-collecting. But it is the only way we know how to get where we want to go. When we find out we can walk, we do our best, but sometimes we're in a hurry to reach a goal. Or we're too tired to toddle. Crawling seems easier. At least it is more familiar. So we revert to a form with which we feel more comfortable and in control. And yet we are born to walk and run, and yearn to experience the freedom to do so.

The Apostle Paul knew that he had to grow and mature into the fullness of who he was:

Not that I have already obtained it [resurrection life], or have already become perfect, but I press on in order that I may lay hold of that for which also I was laid hold of by Jesus Christ.   (Phil. 3:12)

He lived and encouraged us all to live in a discipline of saying "no" to the old, familiar and seductive ways, and to offer ourselves to the Lord for the power to make a new choice.

Even so consider ["reckon" in KJV] yourselves to be dead to sin, but alive to God in Christ Jesus. Therefore *do not let sin reign* in your mortal body that you should obey its lusts, and *do not go on presenting the members of your body to sin* as instruments of unrighteousness; but *present yourselves to God* as those alive from the dead, and your members as instruments of righteousness to God.   (Rom. 6:11-13)

Such a discipline is necessarily a daily business. Paul said *"I die daily"* (1 Cor. 15:31).

Jesus has already done it for me:
I **HAVE BEEN CRUCIFIED** with Christ and it is no longer I who live, but Christ lives in me; and the life which I now live in the flesh I live by faith in the Son of God, who loved me, and delivered Himself up for me.   (Gal 2:20)

I must also take responsibility to act to make what He did my own:

Now those who belong to Christ Jesus **HAVE CRUCIFIED** the flesh with its passions and desires. (Gal 5:24)

What emotional balance and rest we can enjoy when we have acknowledged, confessed, and crucified the driving signals of bitterness from the past!

7

Living With an Alcoholic

**(Donna's story,
as she told it to me)**

I grew up in a home where love was expressed with touches. A daily fare of spontaneous hugs and kisses told my heart how my parents felt about me, and made it easy for me to express affection and warmth to others in the same manner.

My husband, Ken, had parents who cared, and he knew they cared, but there were no embraces — no hugs or kisses to write love on the heart of the child. His mother was extremely reserved. His father had been married before, divorced, and Ken was the only child of the second marriage. His father was not a young man and there was little or no play shared with his son. Ken carried the same kind of reserve which had been modeled to him, never allowing his emotions to show, never really sharing his feelings with anyone.

When Ken and I met, he was overwhelmed to find that I wasn't loose sexually. I was still pure, and he was intrigued. We were both shy, and didn't even kiss one another till our third date.

During our courtship we loved to go to the bars to dance. We lived in Wallace, Idaho, a mining town, and it was a basic part of the area's entertainment culture.

141

We spent a lot of dating time together, dancing and drinking. I was crazy about dancing, but wasn't able to consume very much liquor. And at that time alcohol did not appear to be a problem for Ken.

When we were first married, we were separated except for weekends because I was living in my parents' home and working, while Ken was away, attending college. That kind of arrangement may have been better for us financially, but it was too easy to let mom and dad care for me and make my decisions. I was very much attached to my parents, concerned to perform rightly to please them. I was also prone to tune into the problems and anxieties of others and carry their burdens without knowing what to do about them.

My self-image was not at all good. I had never felt good about my appearance. When I was ten years old, my breasts blossomed dramatically and I hated it. I didn't understand the changes in my body. None of the other girls in my class were developing as I was, and I spent a lot of painful, self-conscious time trying unsuccessfully to cover up unwanted breasts and the embarrassing zits on my face.

I had been molested as a child, by male relatives (not my father), and had never felt safe with boys. Though I had enjoyed a generally good relationship with my father, I loved and feared him all at once. Whenever he would give me one of his enthusiastic teddy-bear hugs, the thought would rise, "Could he also do to me as the one who molested me had done?"

Dating (before Ken appeared on the scene) had been a battle royal. I had strongly cultivated the idea that men were no good, only interested in one thing. In my early teens, I even thought seriously about becoming a nun. I wasn't a Catholic, but I thought the nun's habit would hide my body. I never had a relaxed and healthy relationship with boys.

When I met Ken he was gentle and shy and didn't want to "pounce on my bones." I was fearful at first, but he never violated me. When he became my husband, I looked forward to his coming home, but found myself inhibited sexually, which caused me a great deal of unhappiness.

Ken graduated from college, and for the first time we could make our home together in nearby Spokane, Washington, apart from my parents. But Ken was working as a salesman, frequently making overnight trips. I felt lonely and insecure. I got all wrapped up in my job as a dental assistant.

Ken poured himself into selling computers and calculators. I loved my work. But both of us kept late hours and were overly tired when we did have time together. On weekends we'd clean house and do laundry. There was no real sharing, no fun, and our communication was seriously breaking down. I was becoming more vulnerable than I knew.

My boss at work was a smooth male chauvinist who tried to seduce every woman he came in contact with. He was very skilled in his ability to maneuver to make the most of a woman's need for attention, comfort and

affirmation. Naively, I became infatuated with him. At
first it was only spiritual adultery (looking to him for
the affirmation I should have received from Ken, and
sharing with him what I should have shared with my
husband first or only), and then, inevitably, I wound
up in bed with him. The affair lasted only a short time.

One day, when I was on my way to meet him, I
heard a voice, *"Satan, get behind me."* I stopped my car
and turned around. I broke the relationship with my
boss, and was consequently placed in another position
in the office. A short time later I developed bronchial
pneumonia, had to miss two weeks of work, and a new
girl was put in my place.

When Ken first heard of my infidelity, he was
crushed. His first thought was to divorce me, and then,
"I love you — let's work it out." We tried, but our
efforts were superficial. We understood nothing of how
we were driven by deep roots of fear and insecurity
at the heart level.

We moved several times to towns in the Spokane area
and back again as Ken continued his sales work. We
started thinking about having a family, and Gregg was
conceived. By this time, we had our own home. And
then an aunt came to live with us.

Gregg was born and the aunt stayed on. I desperately
wanted to tell her how I felt about her lack of neatness,
her dating habits, and especially about our need to be
alone with our new baby. But I couldn't, and I was
deeply frustrated and unhappy.

Ken was working with a fellow who had just lost his wife. Trying to be his buddy, he went drinking with him one evening. The next day when I picked up Ken's clothes and shook them, his wedding ring fell out of his pocket. I was devastated!

Ken explained that they had gone to a night club, danced, and he had taken his ring off so people would think he was single. He swore it would never happen again. I wanted to believe him but was not at rest about it.

Soon after that Ken left his sales job and went to work for a savings and loan company in Coeur d' Alene, Idaho. He lived for a while in a tiny house there, until a place large enough for our family could be secured. (By this time, our second child, Laurel, had been born.) I returned with the children to my parents' home in Wallace for that period of time. I didn't like being separated from Ken. I wanted to be with him. And I was always fearful that he might be out drinking with someone. It was a tremendous relief when our family was finally together again, but my anxieties about the drinking were soon aggravated.

Ken had been given an expense account and was told to socialize — to become involved in groups such as the Elks' Club, Rotary, and Jaycees, to foster accounts. As I have said, drinking was a cultural thing, a way of life. Socializing was built around it. We didn't drink at home, but we did whenever we went out together.

The organizations that Ken became a part of would frequently have special men's nights. I was extremely uncomfortable with this. I kept thinking,

"Why is he always out with the boys, drinking?"
"I'm alone, and he doesn't care."
"He'll come home drunk, expect to make love, and I'll feel used, violated."
And when he fulfilled my expectations,
"He smells like booze."

It triggered my childhood memories and feelings of disgust and fear about sex, and reactivated every anger and judgment I had made on men from the beginning of my life. I struggled with my feelings, but I was still fairly well able to control my responses and maintain some stability.

With two children to care for I was busy, and was experiencing an identity and contentment with them I had never felt before. I went with Ken to parties, and we were, at least on the surface, very compatible. From the world's limited perspective, we were the perfect American family. Ken was very competent in his work. We had material things. We appeared to be happy, complacent, solid.

When Laurel was born, we decided we needed to go to church. We took our two-and-a-half-year-old son to Sunday school, but we didn't stay for the worship services. Our Sunday school teacher was the president of North Idaho College and a stimulating teacher. The Lord started working on us by prompting questions concerning our faith, and we began to grow.

Then we were moved back to the town where we had grown up; Ken was put in the position of manager of a savings and loan company there. Now he was *required* to belong to every social club he could — to make a name in the community. He worked hard at his job and made a great success of it. But in the process, the "thing to do" was to take the guys — associates and clients — out to a bar to talk awhile. Soon it became more than that. Ken began to develop a reward system. He would pour himself into his work, and then reward himself for a hard day's work by stopping at a bar to relax. As time went on, the stops become more frequent and more lingering as Ken became dependent on the system and addicted to the liquor.

Our third child was born, and Ken was doing a *lot* of drinking. How did I feel about it? I was angry!

I felt abandoned! Betrayed!

How could he care about me and the children and be

so oblivious to our needs?

It wasn't fair!

My upset grew to the point that I was so angry with him I hated him! And when I nursed my feelings of hate, I would sometimes wish he would be killed. At least then something would be settled; I wouldn't have to struggle with my anxieties concerning where he was, with whom, and what kind of condition he'd be in when and if he finally got home. I wouldn't have to live with the pressure of the responsibility I felt to cover for his absences in relation to the children. I wouldn't

have to wonder what the neighbors witnessed and thought. I was so full of explosive anger
     I could have punched out lights —
          but I didn't know where or how or who to punch.

I was so full of resentment. I didn't even want Ken to touch me. But when he would finally come in the door I would feel so relieved, we would wind up making love — as if that would take care of everything.

When I was thirty-two-years-old, my dad died. He choked on a piece of meat in a restaurant. I had danced with him a few moments before, and then we sat down to eat. I loved dad and couldn't understand why God took him. How did I feel about it?

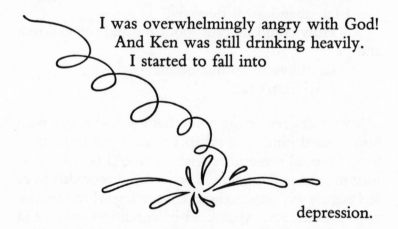

I was overwhelmingly angry with God!
And Ken was still drinking heavily.
I started to fall into

depression.

I chose not to go to church because I always saw dad's casket there (in my mind). I tried to keep my emotions under control. The world would say I should be in control. I decided, "I'll stay home."

I started having female problems, and experiencing substantial fear about the possible consequences of these symptoms.

As I was growing up, I had had my share of operations. Before I was eight, my appendix burst and peritonitis set in. I was traumatized when a drain was put in my stomach with no anesthetic. I had diseased tonsils and suffered terrible earaches; at eleven they took my tonsils out.

After Laurel was born I had a tear in the broad ligament supporting the uterus repaired, and some severe hemorrhoids removed. After Scott, our third child, was born, I had begun to develop female problems, with lots of pain. But now, along with the discomfort and anxiety of that, I was also developing tendonitis in my hands and arms (with tingling and numbness). I remembered how my grandfather had spent twenty-five years in bed with arthritis.

My physical difficulties began to compound and intensify all of my other feelings: fear, anger at Ken, frustration, loneliness, recurring struggles with depression, anger toward God. I was bloated and continually spotting, suffering pain. My uterus was enlarged as though I were four-months pregnant. Intercourse was painful, but tolerated.

My mother tried to comfort me concerning what we knew was unavoidable surgery, but I was unconsolable. I wasn't ready to face the fact that I would never be able to have another child. Even more disturbing was my confused but prevailing belief that I would be nothing but a shell following a hysterectomy. An undesirable neuter. I had never liked being a girl. I had never really felt like a woman. I had always had a struggle with femininity, but I had dared to dream and hope.

The dreaded day arrived, and when I awoke from the anesthetic I felt like something tremendously vital had been taken from me, and I could never get it back. Though I had never really been able to embrace my femininity, now even the possibility seemed to be irrevocably stolen, and I was devastated. I foolishly chose not to move at all in the hospital bed, and developed pneumonia as a result. People visited me and I wept uncontrollably. I was horribly embarrassed, but had no ability to stop.

When I was released from the hospital I went to stay for a time with my mom and grandma. At the time it seemed a reasonable and practical thing to do until I was well again. Ken had to go to work. And I couldn't depend on him to be home in the evenings. What I understand now is that I had never left home emotionally.

I had never individuated, never become my own person. Therefore, I had never really invited or allowed the kind of loving nurture and protection that God designed a husband to provide. I lost a lot of weight, and began to experience a measure of happiness with being thin. I was intrigued with my new figure, but I was tormented by:

the pain from the surgery,

unhealed emotional pain and fear from my prior life,

and the pressure to *"keep* thin." I kept telling myself not to eat.

Ken and I bought a house in Silverton, a suburb of Wallace, in 1961. I loved it, but soon found that a house does not make a home. Ken became very much involved with the Elks Club, which was the hub of the Wallace social life. There were many nights when he didn't come home.

After his day's work there was the irresistible call of bowling and drinking with his men friends. I was stuck at home with three kids! I thought, "He doesn't care!" "He's having fun blowing money we don't have!" It went on and on! I finally hit rock bottom emotionally. My nerves were shot. I was depressed, and I went to see my doctor.

He prescribed tranquilizers.

I took more than he prescribed.

When I had to think and I didn't want to think —
I took a pill.

They made me sleepy. I'd go into a blank state
or take a nap.....

And I had little children at home. I can't remember clearly.

I struggled unsuccessfully to maintain my home. My mother offered to help me clean my house, and I couldn't even feel grateful. I was angry with myself that I couldn't do it.

We were going to church again. We knew we needed something.

But I became more and more involved in all sorts of busy work,

trying to earn my salvation.

I was a fragmented person — tired — depressed — and manipulating, trying to pull all my pieces together.

I remember a chair in the family room with clothes strewn over it.

I had taken a pill. Or was it two?
There were lots of dirty dishes piled carelessly on the counter and in the sink. Newspapers on the floor.

I was so tired — so down under.

How could I begin to make sense of the mess?

Heavy. Mountain of confusion. Couldn't live with it.

"How can I pick it up?"

I saw a tiny piece of paper.

I focused on that tiny item.

"How could I do it?" I could do it by not looking at the whole mess, but by doing one little thing at a time.

That was the beginning of a new beginning.

In this time period John and Paula Sandford came to Wallace to pastor our church. One afternoon John said to me, "When I first saw you I knew you were depressed." I was afraid of John. For one thing, he seemed to have X-ray eyes. I was sure he could see through me — including all my sins and problems.

Another reason I was afraid of John was that I saw him as a father figure. I had been afraid of my father who was usually as gentle as a lamb, but when he was stimulated to anger, he had a violent temper. He'd explode and then get over it quickly. I loved him. But striving to avoid those fifteen seconds of anger kept me in line. I had always worked hard to perform well so he wouldn't yell. When I saw John Sandford he represented fatherly authority. He frightened me, and I thought I would have to tread lightly.

One night, after choir practice, I was in the hall at the church, heading for the door. John called from his office,

"Who's that?"

"Donna."

"Come on in. Let's talk, visit awhile."

"It's late."

But I went into his office and we talked about families and kids. I thought to myself, "Be careful. Keep at a distance. I think he *may* be okay." The evening's conversation started the healing process that followed through many talks and prayers in the following months and years.

Ken's drinking continued. Our children were growing older and were no longer dependent on me. I had felt much more comfortable and confident about raising babies. Some friends of ours at church, Larry and Jean Hansen, were very happily participating in the foster parent program and I became excited about following their example. I could take care of children who needed lots of love and prayers. I could help them, serve God and make a little money at the same time! Maybe I was still trying to win my way to heaven — I couldn't say for sure. What I know without a doubt is that my becoming a foster parent gave me a whole new meaning in life.

My first foster child was a teenager. Ideal fantasies I had entertained about what it meant to be a foster parent were exploded right away. She was messy, a terrible student, and was always testing me. I had to be constantly alert to keep from being caught in her mental and emotional traps.

She was always picking up those whom I judged to be cruddy characters to bring home with her, and much of my time was spent striving to point out to her a better way of life. I was in despair to think that she was sleeping with her boyfriend. I became so overly involved with her that when I became aware that I was no longer talking with my own children, I told the state that I would from that time forth be available to care for children from birth to three years of age only. With them I could feel somewhat in control.

I loved every baby who came into my home! I was safe with them, and felt tremendously fulfilled as I carried them around, rocked them, kissed their cheeks, nibbled on their ears, and prayed healing for their little wounded spirits. Many would come to my arms with tension causing them to be stiff as little ironing boards, and I rejoiced as they relaxed and learned to receive love. It was difficult to let them go, but at the same time satisfying to know that I had been able to prepare their hearts for the nurture of adoptive parents. I had also found some positive identity for myself in the healing of babies.

Ken was drinking more heavily. Our sex life was deteriorating, but I was actually relieved, because he smelled so bad when he was full of alcohol.

Again and again I would prepare a big dinner and he wouldn't come home. I was angry! Why should I have worked so hard for nothing?! "I could have fixed a *simple* meal for the kids!" I would put his dinner in the refrigerator. Then I'd throw the dinner away.

My negative emotions were steadily building, and my health and body were deteriorating in proportion to the stress of my resentments. Arthritis was causing me a lot of pain. I had endless migraine headaches. Sometimes the migraines would put me out of commission for three days. Our oldest son, Gregg, would take over caring for the kids and fixing meals so I could go to bed.

Finally I lost what ability I had to suppress my feelings. When Ken would come home drunk I would lose control. We'd have yelling fights that would wake the kids.

"Don't come to bed! You smell bad!"
"You always wake me up and I can't go back to sleep!"

So Ken would go to sleep on the couch.

My mother died in 1968. In counseling I discovered that she was still ruling my life because I had never cut free. I had never done what the Bible says, "Listen, O daughter, give attention and incline your ear; forget your people and your father's house: then the King will desire your beauty"(Ps. 45:10,11a). It wasn't just Ken's drinking that was keeping us apart. We weren't *cleaving* to one another in a mutually nurturing, one-flesh relationship because there hadn't been any *leaving* of mother and father on my part to make that possible. (Gen. 2:24, Eph. 5:31).

When my father had died I had felt like I had to take his place. I was always in the middle and torn between Ken and my mother. I couldn't be everything to each of them. I took their pain into myself and tried to be what each one wanted, and was totally frustrated. My mother was sick and I constantly had to take her to the doctor.

Ken wasn't very often there for me, so I'd take vengeance on him by rewarding myself with periodic shopping sprees. When I was in need and Ken wasn't comforting me, I'd call my mom, and we'd take little Bill (a foster baby we adopted) and go to Spokane to spend the day spending money. I wouldn't tell Ken when or where we had gone. I felt guilty in a way, but I didn't care. Our home life was gone.

There was no real satisfaction in vengeance-taking. I tried to fill the void by dieting so I might be more appealing. It was almost like selling my body to make

Ken come home. Then I would binge and tell myself the world needs fat people. I felt like I was a yo-yo.

I spent countless hours looking out the window waiting for Ken to come home.

"Why is he drinking, spending money?"

"Who is he with?"

"He's not interested in my anymore. There must be someone he likes better than me."

"Why am I here? What am I good for?"

How could I support four kids if I left?"

I felt trapped. I couldn't leave. I had nowhere to go. No parents to run home to.

I was still going to John Sandford for counseling, trying to let Jesus get at the root causes for my problems. And Ken and I went Tuesdays at noon to the Sandfords for Bible study. In 1966 I received the baptism of the Holy Spirit.

I was trying to change:
   going for counseling faithfully,
     working to keep my house clean,
       preparing good meals,
         being as dutiful as I knew how.

I was trying to do what John Sandford said to edify my husband. I would make love to make Ken feel better. And sometimes it was the best ever! Ken's inhibitions were lowered and he was a better lover. But sometimes I couldn't get beyond, "Why does he have to be drunk like this?" I felt violated again. I was never free from the pain of arthritis and the migraine headaches.

One day John said,

"Donna, will you give up your depression?"

"I don't know. Why?"

"You'll never be well if you don't."

"I'm afraid."

"Will you do it for the love of the Lord?"

"Yes. It's okay. I believe the Lord will always be there."

John prayed for me. I felt like I was in a black hole and John was reaching in to pull me out. I focused on the Lord. John placed the cross between me and the depression. I was angry at John. He had taken the depression away from me and I couldn't go back in there to hide. The cross was there and I had to face what was outside that which had been my miserable, but familiar blackness.

I had developed some warm emotional feelings for John. He was sympathetic — hearing, and giving compassion and love. I thought, "My, this is a marvelous man." (I was in a transference relationship.) John was everything I couldn't see in Ken. But John kept carefully focusing me on the Lord all the time.

After my born-again experience, with the baptism of the Holy Spirit, I would look intently at my favorite picture of Jesus, and imagine what it would be like to feel His robe, touch His beard. Jesus met me there in that child-like focus, called me beyond my picture, and made himself real to me.

Ken started going to John for counseling. Ken had experienced sexual union with two different women while he was drinking, and John said he should share that with me. I didn't receive his confession very well. I had somehow managed to forget my past sins, feeling only that Ken had violated me. He had given away what was mine. I believe I had known in my spirit he had done it, and now it was, in a sense, a relief to know. At the same time, I went into an emotional tailspin.

"How did I measure up? Did I perform as well as they?"

Ken replied, "It meant nothing. I was drunk. It got out of control."

His attempts to reassure me helped very little. I couldn't separate sex and love!

All kinds of advice about sex were coming out in the newspapers and TV media. Do this or that to experience fullness in sex. I asked myself, "Do I hear bells? Do I have climaxes?" I thought, "Maybe I should experiment with some of the things they're talking about. Maybe I have to do these things so Ken won't want other women."

I had lost my battle to stay thin. My figure was chunky and I was striving with any diet. I tried every diet that came along! I couldn't feel beautiful. There was my tummy — the paunch, the pounds and the stretch marks. I would begin to feel depressed, but I couldn't fall into it. I talked to God all the time. I asked questions constantly. John would often answer my questions with, "You're working the putty again. Quit it." So I went to God with most of my questions.

Ken was still out drinking, and I was trying to get answers. Sometimes I would ask him my questions, and he would try to answer, but he met fireballs of energy in me, coming from a hot boiling pot. No man can deal with that. Ken would respond by leaving.

I'd feel, "I'm rejected — alone with the kids — I need answers — I'm going to God" And I'd cry out, "God, are you listening?!"

During that time my walk with God started to take hold. Important issues started coming into place, the hard way. I *had* to put everything on the Lord. I'd start to say, "I trust you, God," but I knew my heart wasn't in it. "I'll trust you anyway." I got hold of the book *Prison to Praise.* AND I DID IT!

— In spite of everything getting worse — and I had to keep starting again. . . . . and again and. . .
I had to GRAB for help and hope.
Counseling helped.
I held onto precious moments.

The fact was, we were a dysfunctional family, co-dependent.

For me, pain far outweighed sexual excitation or emotion. It was hard on Ken and made him vulnerable to quasi-affairs connected with his drinking. Occasionally he would go to "whorehouses" with buddies — just to party and drink. The houses would sometimes hold "good will" parties to entertain anyone in the business community who wanted to come.

The madam would send generous contributions to civic projects and fund drives such as the March of Dimes. Donations were even sent to churches occasionally. My fear was always that Ken might succumb to sexual temptation while he was partying in that environment.

I was angry! I looked for little ways to poke fun at Ken, to belittle him in front of the kids. I wouldn't set his place at the table. With impassioned disdain, I would announce, "If he doesn't come home, we won't worry about it." I was vindictive and moody, and the kids were suffering.

At the same time, our family went to church, served on the deacons' and trustees' boards, sang in the choir, went to Bible study — and went on outings with the Sandford family. We looked righteous on the outside, but we were a mess on the inside.

The Sandfords moved away from Wallace in December, 1973, in response to the Lord's direction to establish Elijah House, a non-denominational ministry of writing, counseling and teaching.

In the spring of 1978 my arthritis had progressed to such a degree that I had to have my spine scraped and fused in two places due to large calcium deposits. My bone structure was weakened and there was nerve damage.

Later, surgery was done through my throat to remove a spur on my neck, and at that time a piece of bone was taken from my thigh to reinforce my neck. Still later, surgery was done on my wrists because of growths which caused numbness in my fingers and seriously handicapped the use of my hands. I was flat on my back with severe pain from the top of my head to my toes. I lived round the clock on Tylenol 4 with codeine.

Depression was threatening again. I had no answers. Ken was getting worse. Our kids were growing up, and leaving. Our personal finances were terrible. Ken and I had no sexual relationship; we were just existing together. I felt so alone!

On weekends I felt safer; Ken didn't go out to drink on weekends. I tried to cram everything into those two days! Grab hold like it's the whole of life! I knew Ken wouldn't come home on Monday night.

I was flat on my back in pain. I couldn't focus. I couldn't get out of my house.

I kept talking to God, "Will it be like this forever?" "When will there be hope?"

We hired a housekeeper.

After two years of constant pain, I was still unable to negotiate with freedom. I wanted to go back to church. The pain pills helped me to function limitedly, but my balance was impaired due to stiffness. By this time I was calling out to God,

"I want to die! Take me home! Let Ken be responsible for the kids (grown by now). He can eat at restaurants and do the laundry at the laundromat."

I didn't have the courage to die. One day as I was trying to clean our bird cage (and I couldn't stand up to clean it), I said, "Okay, God — heal me or I'll go to bed and I'll stay there and never get up again!"

A short time later a friend called to tell me that Billy Graham was coming to Albi Stadium in Spokane, and the planning committee needed homes where prayer meetings could be held to prepare for the crusade. She thought it would be good for me to be involved, and she also knew that my housekeeper cleaned my house on Saturday. It would still be in good order for a meeting on Monday, and all I would have to do was to plug in a pot of coffee and have a plate of cookies ready.

I agreed to do it. I fortified myself with pain pills so I could attend an instructional meeting in Coeur d' Alene. There I found out that hosting a prayer meeting would involve more than I had bargained for. I was expected to canvass my neighborhood! Every home in Silverton had multiple steps leading to the front door. Because of the arthritic pain I could hardly take ten steps on level ground without resting.

I said, "There is no way I can canvass. That lets me out."

My friend said, "We will do it. You host, and I'll canvass."

"Okay."

Later the woman called to say she couldn't do it. I thought, "What'll I do? If I don't follow through, I'll let God down. How can He forgive me?"

A few days later the pastor of the church we were then attending in nearby Kellogg called to tell me that Idaho Falls was holding a charismatic conference, and he felt it was important for me to go. I had already been in every healing line available, and nothing had happened. But Ken agreed to take me — then had to cancel at the last minute. I went ahead with two people from our church.

I arrived stiff and full of pain. When they called people forward for prayer, I wouldn't go. They called my name, "Donna Campbell." They prayed for me, and nothing happened. How could I possibly canvass my neighborhood? I said to the Lord, "I don't know how I'll do it, God. You'll have to do it for me."

The day of the canvass arrived. I said to Ken, "Please pray with me for strength to make some calls." He prayed for me, and I told God, I want to do this for you. I will have to depend on you and trust."

I started out into my neighborhood at 10:00 a.m. Before the day was finished I had canvassed thirty-two houses, and had walked up and down stairs at each! Before that day I hadn't even been able to go downstairs to our own basement!

I was exhausted, and I had a lot of pain. I lay down for two or three minutes. And suddenly I realized THERE WAS NO MORE PAIN!

"MY GOD, I'VE BEEN HEALED!" I was crying, singing, thanking God, all at once. God had worked a miracle — in me!

Ken had left the banking business to go into real estate; he was running two offices and doing very well when disaster hit the Silver Valley. A large corporation had purchased a leading silver-lead and zinc mine and smelter in the area, bled the company, and then closed it down. This caused the shutdown of many smaller mines which could not afford to send ore to far-away smelters.

The price of silver was low at the time, and lumber, the area's other primary industry, was also having problems. The economy of the area plummeted radically, and real estate could scarcely be given away. Ken struggled as long as he could, finally lost his business, and was forced to declare bankruptcy. He was devastated and humiliated. He had failed.

His business losses affected the welfare of friends and associates who had depended on him, and there was no way he could make it up to them. His life was a loss and a disappointment to his family, friends and God — he was a drinker, an adulterer — rotten. He pummeled himself emotionally again and again, "Why didn't Donna leave me years ago?" Ken started crying out to God sincerely from the bottom of the black hole he had fallen into.

We lost our home and had to leave the Valley; we got as far as Coeur d'Alene. I was hired as a maid in a country club, and later worked in the deli at K-Mart. Ken worked awhile at selling real estate and life insurance. His mother helped us financially, and we received some state aid for one child under eighteen.

Food-stamps were helpful. And I received some SSI funds for disability. (I still moved with considerable stiffness, and had to work with residual numbness in my hands). We began to experience tremendous growth in the Lord.

It was a relief to leave the Valley. I rejoiced to think that Ken wouldn't get hooked up with his old drinking buddies. We found a two-bedroom apartment. And then one night Ken got drunk, and I was devastated! It was starting all over!

I felt anger — disgust — frustration — desperation...

He was sending money we didn't have! How could he?

I confronted him, "I'm working, bringing in money regularly — why not *you?!*"

Ken's breaking and crushing was coming to a head.

Ken was brought home by the police at 5:00 one morning. He had been given a DUI citation; his driver's license was taken away and he wasn't allowed to drive at all at night. I thought, "This will curtail his drinking. Praise God!"

But two and a half blocks away from our apartment was a pub. He could easily walk there. The pattern started again. Ken was sleeping on the couch, and I was getting up early in the morning to go to work. However, Ken's drinking at this point was not at all what it had been before. He only went on an occasional drunk.

Ken had to serve his weekend in jail, and God did something during that time. I never questioned Ken about it. I knew that the Lord had somehow gotten through to him, because things began to change. From that time on there was no more going out to drink. No friends to drink with. No money. But we were happy! We began to talk and share.

Then Ken suffered a major heart attack. That was the last stage of the breaking Ken had to go through. He was in intensive care for six weeks. (Years prior to this he had said, "If you could lock me up, Lord, for six weeks, I could lick this habit.") The Lord had honored his request.

While Ken lay there in the hospital I realized how very much I really loved him. I couldn't stand the thought of losing him! The tremendous accumulation of anger, frustration, and self-righteousness in me was dealt a death blow and I began to see our relationship in a totally different perspective. I prayed earnestly from the very depths of my being, "Lord, spare his life. You surely have something much better planned for our lives than we have known or seen."

KEN'S HEART WAS HEALED! I'm talking about both physical and emotional/spiritual healing. Not only that, but his drinking and smoking (several packs a day) stopped without a single withdrawal problem!

In the timing of the Lord, we joined the Elijah House staff. I answer the phone and greet counselees, do some crisis praying and counseling on the phone, schedule appointments for people who come from all over the world to receive ministry from our staff of trained Christian counselors. I also answer a portion of the mail that comes to Elijah House — the kind that seeks answers to questions about marriage and family problems, or referrals to reading materials, or people who can provide help in their local areas, etc.

In 1988, I hand-wrote 697 such replies, and in 1989, 775. 1990's count will surely surpass previous years. I have spent hours at the copier, have run miles up and down stairs and have enjoyed hosting Elijah House Board and Staff meetings in that part of Elijah House that Ken and I now call home.

God is putting Ken's business, banking and real estate skills and experience to work for Him as Ken serves as Elijah House President and Business Manager. Ken coordinates the work of fourteen staff people, in addition to scheduling the Sandfords' teaching throughout the world.

He supervises the maintenance of the ministry property, and, with the Board, seeks the Lord's practical direction for the working out of the vision God originally gave the Sandfords. John and Paula Sandford say they can now travel with confidence that everything at home is running well. And I am proud of my husband!

The Lord's breaking time for Ken and myself spanned thirty-four years. I was twenty-two when I fell into adultery; I was fifty-six by the time we had dealt with all of this. I wouldn't want to go through any of it again, but I wouldn't take a million dollars for the experience we've had.

Ken knows that he had been depending on many other things rather than God, and the Lord, in His judgment and mercy, has taken everything away. I know that I cannot afford to nurse any kind of resentment even for a moment. All that the locusts ate during those years has been restored far beyond anything I could describe (Joel 2:25). God is merciful and He is faithful.

I am now able to control my weight in healthy ways, watching what I eat because I care for my body as a temple of the Holy Spirit. The only medication I take now is anti-inflammatory. I have no need for tranquilizers or pain killers.

When stresses come into our life, we release them to the Lord, in prayer. When irritations come, I know I am responsible for my responses, and I pray, "Show me my sin. God, be more in my life." My image of myself is much better than it ever was because it is based on an identity I have in Christ which I don't have to strive to maintain or defend.

Ken and I carry a measure of grief for our children, for what they have suffered. But we know we are forgiven, and we've been able to release them to God and allow them to take their own responsibility before Him. We believe that as we have been healed and continue to grow in the Lord, the blessing of God that He designed to flow through parents will reach our children more and more purely and powerfully.

The enemy wants us to get hung up on guilt. We know that we are not to focus on the past. We have fully acknowledged our past and have repented for it. Now we are to focus on the redemptive power of the Lord.

I can't describe my present feelings — fantastic — great — I can't find adequate words. I know God gives me divine power to cope. It hurts to forgive. I can and must always choose to forgive, but I can't make it happen. That's the Lord's job. Our relationship is much deeper and more wonderful than we ever thought possible. I belong to God. Ken belongs to God.

Every day as I answer the phone from my desk at Elijah House, and find myself talking to hurting women whose husbands are addicted to drink, and who are into adultery, I say,

"I've been through it. You CAN be healed."

ANNA'S STORY — Remembrances From Her Childhood

(Anna is a real person, a friend of mine, and I tell her story as she told it to me. But I have changed her name at her request.)

There is a great deal that I can't remember clearly about my childhood — partly because I'm in my seventies now, partly because I suppressed a lot that was painful when I was a little girl, and largely because I've experienced a great deal of healing over the years.

My dad was an alcoholic, though he never admitted it. Mother said he was always a drinker. He was so sensitive to liquor he could get tipsy from just smelling it. All of his sisters were alcoholics, and his brother might have followed in the family line had it not been for his strong Baptist beliefs.

Mother always covered for dad. He could be falling-down-sloppy drunk, and she would say he had a bad headache, or tell us that he wasn't home yet because there was a cow in the ditch. If he fell out of his chair at the dinner table, she would quietly get him to the bedroom. But she always acted as if everything were fine, and no one ever talked about it.

We just went on with what we were doing as if nothing had happened. I would pretend he wasn't drunk. There was never a Christmas or Easter or any other holiday when daddy wasn't sloppy drunk. He would disappear somewhere, and the rest of the family would go on and celebrate without him as if everything were okay. I guess my mother thought it was easier to stoically ignore the problem than to make an issue of it, with a husband who lived in complete denial. I know that I keyed off of her and developed strong habits of suppressing my feelings.

Daddy was never physically abusive to our family. He adored my mother. Their family backgrounds were quite different. He had grown up on a farm. She had been well-educated in music in Chicago, had sung with Lilly Pons, and was ready to make her own professional singing debut when she met and fell in love with my father. If anyone had challenged her choice at that time with a question such as, "What's wrong with your young man?" her reply would certainly have been something like, "What's wrong with a piano bench?"

Daddy thought of himself as a self-made man. In many ways he was a good, moral man. He called himself a Christian. He was the head usher and an elder at church. But at home he was often a drunk fallen into cow manure in our barn with a bottle in his mouth.

Relating to him was like relating to two totally different people. Sober, he could be charming and lovable. Drunk, I couldn't stand him! I didn't *like* him at all, and that bothered me. I prayed about it and the Lord told me it was okay, so long as I *loved* him. Today I still can't stand for anyone not to be what they claim to be!

My father was horribly abusive to animals! He must have been taking out all of his frustrations and animosities on them. He would viciously kick our dogs for no apparent reason. And our cows always had broken tails. How did that happen? He would be angry, grab a tail, and twist it till it snapped!

One memory remains extremely vivid in my mind. I was about eight years old. I walked into the barn and caught my father pitchforking one of our cows! I was so angry I grabbed the pitchfork out of his hands, stood between him and the cow, and shouted, "You get out of here and go away or I'll ram this thing through your body!"

When I was older, once again I stood between him and the animals, and this time I knocked him down in ferocious anger! I didn't like knocking my father down, but when he was drunk and abusive, I couldn't see him as "father." There was such a radical change in his personality. I felt like I was shoving someone else — a completely different person who was a threat to us all, and had to be stopped by somebody.

I can remember so many times watching my father go into the barn and then come out like a man with no bones, disintegrated in front of my eyes. How did I feel?

Confused...wondering...hurting...

If I was ashamed, I didn't know it. —
         My mother never quivered an eyelash.
I wasn't consciously afraid. Perhaps anger overwhelmed my fear.

Everywhere we went I was *glad* he wasn't with us!

After I grew older my father insisted that he had quit drinking altogether. But he continued to go on "trips" and I knew he was still in bondage to liquor. My suspicions were confirmed as I was working in his garden one day and found bottles of wine, whiskey, and canned heat stashed in the ground among the flowers. I could never trust him or rest in him.

How Did All of This Affect My Life?

In relation to drinking I have been very careful not to get something started that I can't handle. I know that

I am probably as vulnerable to alcohol as anyone else in my family and I choose not to go that way.

I have always had a problem with stress. I'm gifted with a lot of creativity and I enjoy doing many things. But I tend to become too involved. I take on too much emotional responsibility, and then I suffer from severe headaches, and rashes all over my body.

Marriage was for me a series of disappointments and disasters. When my youngest daughter was about eight or nine I had a nervous breakdown and was given shock treatments. Healing began to happen after those shock treatments, but my doctor told me it was my faith that made me well. I still have occasional bad dreams that relate to the fear I experienced during those treatments. And I can't watch space movies like "Star Trek" and enjoy them, because of the flashing lights and sounds that activate that memory.

I love the Lord, and He has worked faithfully, even miraculously at times, to heal me. Once I was expected to die, and surprised everyone, including my physician, with a radical and "impossible" recovery. God must have more to do with me here on earth.

My daughter has always been a healing gift to me from God. She never really seemed like a child. As a small child and all the time she was growing up she had a special quality of wisdom, empathy and sympathy that she lovingly gave to me. I searched to find a good church where I could relate in a close, personal way to the Lord and His people.

When my daughter married, she and her husband ministered deeply to me. I don't remember what happened when they prayed for me — I think I passed out — but it was powerful! After that I began to drink gulps of healing and experience bundles of goodness. I also had a vivid spiritual experience of sitting on God's lap. No person had ever held me like that.

I am grateful for the abundance of healing I have experienced. But God isn't finished with me yet. In His wisdom He has left me with a barometer and provided me with protection of loved ones. When too many activities and concerns have been stimulating me, sparking my sensitive and overworked nervous system, tension builds, and I begin to experience a kind of frantic urgency to control my world.

I pay attention to the symptoms and retreat to the quietness of my room. There I can spend private restorative time with my heavenly Father who is consistently and reliably the same strong, understanding, gentle and nurturing person yesterday, today, and always. And when I fail to heed the signals, my family, with a loving and gentle sternness, reminds me, "Grandma, it's time to go to your room."

For my father and my mother have forsaken me, but the LORD will take me up.   (Ps. 27:10)

The Lord is for me among those who help me . . .
                                    (Ps. 118:7a)

8
Singles' Searches, Sorrows and Solaces

Brenda worked for our ministry at Elijah House for several years. She was a beautiful, intelligent, insightful young woman in her thirties who profoundly blessed many with her gifts of counseling and prayer. Almost everyone was puzzled by the fact that she remained single.

She had a lovely face and figure, and her shiny auburn hair would have well qualified her to pose for shampoo commercials. She dressed tastefully and attractively. Her bright personality was charming. She was conversant on a wide variety of subjects. Several counselees commented that they couldn't understand why men weren't lined up at her door.

I'm not describing a super-woman who possessed an unflawed personality with whom no one could identify. Like the rest of us, there were wounds in her heart to be healed, habits yet to be transformed. At that time there was a privateness about her which did not allow many to know her intimately. But neither was there a sign on her forehead telling people to remain at a distance.

Because Brenda was an excellent teacher, and as a single could identify with the feelings of singles, we asked her to address the singles' issues at a seminar. I will never forget the response she received when she stated emphatically, "There *is* life after puberty!" From the audience erupted waves of laughter through pain. And the people settled in to hear Brenda's message which said again and again in many ways that our basic security, wholeness, value and effectiveness as persons — whether we are married or single — depends upon our developing relationship with the Lord Jesus Christ.

It is He who gives power to confront and overcome the hurtfull and/or crippling circumstances of life; it is He who is able to transform weaknesses to strengths and deserts to gardens. Though you may be single, having many attendant struggles and frustrations, you are not rejected and you are never alone.

Brenda is now a happily married wife and mother, and continues to counsel in another state from an ever-expanding and deepening base of trust in God. She is not a whole person because she has found a marriage partner. She is able to be a good partner in marriage because she is becoming more and more whole in Christ.

HEART-CRIES FROM HURTING SINGLES
"I'm past forty — my time-clock is running out. My chances of becoming a mother are fading fast."

Most women who share this cry simply endure the disappointment and develop ways of coping. Some become loving "aunts" or "best grown-up friends" to their friends' children. Our children were not able to be with their own natural grandparents very often because they lived hundreds of miles away. But they were always blessed by surrogate grandmothers in the church who took delight in loving them.

Some single women become gifted teachers or youth workers. God can find many ways to enable a barren woman to become the joyful mother of children (Ps. 113:9). If you have already "adopted" and nurtured many children and still find an empty ache rising from deep inside — an unsatisfied longing for your *own* — know that your feelings are normal. God understands, and wants to comfort your heart.

The natural desire in a woman to bring forth life is so powerful that today increasing numbers of single women around the world are deliberately becoming pregnant because of their overwhelming desire to mother a child. Often they have been so wounded, rejected and hardened that they care very little about whose seed they receive. They never intended to live in a sustained covenant relationship with the father.

For them, the pain of barrenness is so intense that they choose to bring a baby into the world for the sake of their own comfort and fulfillment with no consideration for the deep wounding this can inflict on the spirit of their baby. Every child needs both a father and a mother. Children so conceived begin life with a seed of rejection and a sense of being used.

Until those wounds are healed, they will be crippled in their ability to receive the love the mother felt she was so desperate to give. And until the mother's self-centered motives are discovered by her, repented of, and forgiven, the quality of love she tries to express will be seriously warped by its self-serving nature.

"I grieve for the loss of my babies — the ones I've never had — as if they had been born and died!"

I nearly wept as I heard this cry. Here was a lovely woman, just past forty. She was attractive, a rare mixture of gentleness and strength. Her life had been invested for years in a ministry which brought people to life, and she had learned well the meaning of love in spending herself for the sake of others.

There was no question that she had become the mother of many spiritual children. But she was grieving for her *own*. My heart broke for her as I identified with her sense of loss. She had truly conceived in her imagination and labored to bring forth her children in the deep longing of her dreams, but they were stillborn, and she had never held them in her arms. She was fearful she never would.

She was trying not to be angry, but the thought kept coming to her, "What a waste that I have all this reproductive equipment inside of me! What a useless bother to live through biological cycles that produce nothing but discomfort!" I kept thinking what a fine mother she could be, and wondering what had happened to the husband God may have intended for her. "O God, if he is out there somewhere, let them find one another quickly."

"I love the Lord. I love my work. I have lots of friends. But I always wanted to have my own family. There's an empty place in me that nothing really satisfies."

This is the complaint we have heard most often from women serving as singles on the mission field. They are usually attractive, talented and dedicated women who would not be satisfied with ordinary jobs which would simply bring them a paycheck. They sincerely want to invest their lives in serving the Lord and setting others free. Most of them feel called by God in some way to do that.

But rarely have we met anyone who would not admit that she had always dreamed of doing the same sort of work alongside a husband, sharing work, play, joys, sorrows and CHILDREN together.

Some on the field were perhaps not first "called" in the sense of God giving them a clear directive to go. It was rather the loss of a husband through death or divorce that propelled them into searching for meaningful places to invest their lives. God then met them where they were and opened a door. But they still feel a personal need for love with skin on it.

There are women who choose from the beginning to invest their lives in careers rather than in nurturing a family. They become so busy and pour themselves so completely into becoming successful businesswomen, decorators, teachers, scientists or journalists, etc., that for years they pay no attention to what lies hidden beneath their conscious focus.

Then as retirement years approach, they begin to recognize that there is a part of them that has never had a chance to live. Some seem to be content to remain as they are. Others find their successes and laurels painfully lacking in human warmth. One brilliant and talented single woman pointed to her PhD certificate framed on the wall of her study, and said to me with tears in her eyes, "As I grow older I'm having a terrible time trying to cuddle up to that."

"I get so hungry for touch! I'm not even talking about
    sex (though that could be a problem) — just touch
— hugs
     — someone to hold me,
      Someone to talk to,
       to go places with,
        to share important things,
        to pray with,
         to grow old with."

The woman who made this comment had been married and had raised several children. But her marriage had ended in divorce, and her children had grown up and moved away. She was fearful that the intensity of her unfulfilled needs might propel her into an inappropriate and/or premature relationship.

At least she was aware of her vulnerability and was seeking help. Many women are not. They are simply driven by feelings which block out discernment. Many more avoid seeking counsel because they fear misunderstanding and condemnation.

Condemnation is entirely inappropriate. Her feelings are natural. Woman was designed by God not only with a *need for* love. She was also created to fulfill her man, to nurture and protect his heart. "The heart of her husband trusts in her, and he will have no lack of gain" (Ps. 31:11). When she is denied that opportunity, she is also denied the expression of a part of who she is. Whether she can identify it clearly or not, her sense of intrinsic worth is damaged.

The single woman who has never been chosen, the single woman who was chosen but lost her husband, and the married woman who was given the promise of being chosen but is shut out of her husband's heart by his inability to be intimate and corporate, all share the same basic hurt and frustration.

They are blocked from becoming all they were created to be. Man and woman were both created for corporateness. But it seems to me that generally speaking, women naturally gravitate more easily to intimacy while men tend to flee.

"Obviously I'm not good looking — no one has chosen me."

This comment tumbled from the mouth of an unusually attractive woman who was just about to celebrate her fortieth birthday. She very capably occupied a position of responsibility in an outstandingly reputable international service organization. People not only treated her with respect and honor; they called her "friend."

But she felt ugly because no man had chosen her as a wife. Though she had dated from time to time, no serious relationship had ever developed. My husband and I tried to affirm her beauty as we could so clearly see it.

She appreciated our effort, but all the persuasive affirmation in the world could not have changed the "facts" which she had identified as truth. No one had chosen her despite her recognized and acknowledged positive attributes. Therefore, in her mind she "knew" no one would choose her because of her appearance.

Possible Answers for Often-Asked Whys

If there is someone out there for me, then why haven't I found him?

Our son Mark was a student at Denver Theological Seminary. Maureen, who did eventually become his wife, lived in Calgary, Alberta. Mark was impatient and somewhat angry because he was almost twenty-nine without having yet found the love of his life. His three brothers had been happily married at 19, 20, and 21. He was glad for their sakes but wondered why he wasn't being so blessed.

Mark had a number of friends who happened to be girls, but no romantic interest developed in the relationships. Family and friends would try to encourage him with, "She's out there somewhere, Mark. I just know it." And he would reply, "I've heard that before and I'd like to believe it!" I was concerned for the growing anger and despair in his attitude, and one day as I was praying for him, the Lord clearly led me to read Psalm 128:2,3:

> When you shall eat of the fruit of your hands, you will be happy and it will be well with you. Your wife shall be like a fruitful vine, Within your house, your children like olive plants around your table.

I copied the Scripture and gave it to Mark, saying I believed that the Lord meant it for him. He carried it in his Bible.

Meanwhile Maureen was watching her twenties passing by quickly, and though she was encouraged to be receiving some healing for early wounds in her life, she also was impatient and frustrated, wondering if she would ever find the right man.

Then my husband, John, went to Calgary to teach, and Maureen was in the audience. She asked God to send her a husband like him.

Awhile later, Janet, who was on our staff at the time, counseled with Maureen, and in the process of their talking together, she happened to mention Mark's name. Maureen knew in her spirit that someday she would marry him. (She didn't know that Mark is in many ways more like John than John is).

Not long after that Maureen attended a course at a church where they were studying our books. They asked her name, and then inquired as to why she had come. She answered, "I'm here because God is preparing me to marry Mark Sandford." The people were a bit startled, but they didn't challenge her. I don't know whether it was because she sounded so confident, or because they thought she was a bit strange.

Maureen came to Coeur d'Alene for counseling. Mark was home, doing an internship with Elijah House at the time. We sent him to meet her plane. Two lost and lonely people were zapped that night — Mark didn't know it, but Maureen did — and they talked till nearly two in the morning. That began a courtship that continued mostly by letter and phone over the nine months that followed.

Maureen came to our home to visit again. She had intended to stay only a short time, but we kept encouraging her to extend her visit. Long before we met Maureen, John had had a dream in which he saw the woman he knew would someday be Mark's wife. But Maureen didn't quite look like the girl in the dream. As John was praying one day he heard a voice saying, "Help me find Mark's heart." He suddenly recognized that the voice he heard, and the woman in the dream were indeed Maureen. Only her hair style was different.

He caught her alone in the study one afternoon and asked her, "How do you feel about Mark? Do you want him to marry you?" Her eyes teared and she said, "Oh, yes." So her future father-in-law prayed with her, but said nothing to Mark.

A day or two later, Mark told us that he had asked Maureen to marry him — "I believe God told me to ask her" — and she had consented. Maureen never returned to Canada. Since their marriage, we have seen both of them blossoming, bringing out the best in one another, and they already have two beautiful olive plants around their table, a girl and a boy, with hope for more.

What is the importance of this story? God's timing! Mark was a late bloomer. He had been molested as a little child. (See *Healing Victims of Sexual Abuse*, published by Victory House.) In him were deep memories that he had totally suppressed. In the first few weeks of their marriage, the Holy Spirit brought those memories to his consciousness.

Maureen also had deep wounds which needed the healing oil of the Lord's Spirit. The Lord's love between them had prepared their hearts to minister to one another. At just the right time in the maturation and healing process, God brought them together. If they had found each other earlier, neither would have been prepared to meet the other sensitively, and issues rising from past wounds would have seriously hindered intimacy. It could have been disaster instead of celebration.

I believe that often when the Lord doesn't seem to be answering the anxious and impatient prayers of His children, it is His kindness and His mercy that holds His answers back. If you are able to risk, and willing to do what you're doing and wait, trusting, He will get you to your life on time.

What if there's something in me that is preventing?

It could very well be that there are blockages in you. Some of the most common are:

1. The woundings you have received.
2. The lies you have accepted.
3. The judgments you have made.
4. The expectations you have developed.
5. The walls you have built.
6. The inner vows you have made.
7. The unconscious messages you send.

And you don't have to continue to live with any of them.

What wounding?

From the time of your conception you have within you a sensitive personal spirit which knows whether you were invited or an accident. You rest in the love that flows easily between your parents, or you tense in fear and hurt in the midst of their quarreling.

You begin early to know yourself as a blessing or an intrusive burden by the way your parents respond to your needs with gratitude or griping. You feel chosen as they delight in being with you, or you are deeply wounded by their neglect or physical and verbal abuse.

As your parents touch you with clean wholesome affection, you are filled with love and strength of spirit to face life. As unconditional love and appropriate discipline are administered together, the question of belonging is settled at deep levels in your spirit. You develop the courage and security to venture, to make mistakes, and try again.

Without these basic gifts of acceptance and nurture, your spirit withers like a plant that receives too little water and sunshine. If you are continually lacerated by criticism, you may curl up and die emotionally, becoming a puddle of rejection, an apology for being. Or you may lash out in hurt and anger and strive either to show them or shame them.

If your mother is a happy, vibrant person who enjoys being a woman, you may easily identify with her and embrace your own femininity. If she is a miserable slob, or if your father treats her like one and she lets him, you may reject her as a model. If your parents, especially your father, tell you as you are growing up that you are gorgeous and they are proud of you, you "know" you are beautiful whether you are or not.

You feel like a treasure and a gift to bless a man's heart. If no one tells you how lovely you are, and what a delight you are, or if primary people insult and ridicule you, you may feel ugly and ashamed though you are built to win beauty contests.

What lies?

That you have no right to be. That you will have to earn love if you are to get any. That you are only worthy of love if you do everything right. That you are a mistake, an intrusion and a burden. That you don't belong. That there is something dreadfully wrong with you. That you are ugly and unchoosable. That you should be rejected. That you are somehow responsible for the sins of your parents and, therefore, you don't really deserve blessing.

What judgments?

It is one thing to recognize the fact of a parent's neglect or abuse, and to acknowledge the wounding in yourself — you may rightly judge something or someone to be immoral, unjust, and hurtful. It is another matter to judge in a condemning way as you wallow in hate and anger. Whether it is expressed overtly or not, such hatred murders the one to whom it is directed.

Judge not, lest you be judged. For *in the way you judge, you will be judged,* and by your standard of measure, it will be measured to you. (Matt. 7:1)

It is true that when you have indulged in hatred and fed your angers over a period of time, you should expect to reap some repetition of hurtful patterns in your life. We are not responsible for the sins of our parents. But we are accountable for the responses that we ourselves make and the attitudes to which we cling, even though we may not remember or be aware that we made such judgments.

What expectations?

That no one will ever really love you, choose you, treat you with sensitivity or fully meet your needs. That you will always have to look out for yourself. That you will do a good job and be criticized anyway. That no one will be able to understand your heart-cries. That you will be passed by. No one will see you or want what you have to offer. No one will value you as a person. That you will probably have to work hard to win a place of belonging, and then be rejected anyway. That there will never be a place for you to rest.

What walls?

When we have been wounded, we learn to build defensive walls to protect our feelings. We harden our hearts and refuse, often unconsciously, to let anyone in beyond a certain point. We may gladly serve others and minister to their wants. As we do that we can preserve some measure of control.

But we maintain ourselves as very private people, hiding our own needs, hurts and fears, because if we open our hearts we become vulnerable to the imperfections of others. We choose the pain of loneliness and isolation rather than risk the possibility of violation or betrayal.

Unfortunately, a wall is a wall. Walls not only keep out the bad. They block out the good as well. Ezekiel 36:26 and 11:19 both say that Jesus will take out of us the "heart of stone" and give us a "heart of flesh." He offers us the protection of His breastplate of righteousness (Eph. 6:14). But we are so afraid of giving up the security of our own defenses that when good times and loving people have begun to melt our hearts, we may suddenly stop in the midst of celebrating new freedoms and fellowships to flee back to our familiar prison.

What vows?

I opened my heart to trust once, and was betrayed. I will *never* trust again.

It hurts to be rejected. I will reject before I am rejected.

I shared my feelings and people used them against me. I will hide my feelings.

My mother was a doormat for my father. I will never let anyone walk on me like that!

Such strong vows made early in life are directives programed into the computers of our inner being. When our "keys" are punched later in life by similar circumstances, out come instructions driving us to respond compulsively.

What unconscious messages?

You don't like me. You won't choose me; no one ever has. You'll reject me. You'll go away; everyone does. I can't trust you. I'll not need you. Go ahead and hit me; I won't cry. I can take care of myself.

What can you do to get rid of the above? (as they apply to you)

James 5:16 says, "Confess your sins to one another, and pray for one another, so that you may be healed."

It is essentially that simple. With others, and then in personal discipline:

Pray:

   1) that the Lord will pour His love into the depths of the spirit of the wounded child you have been, and cause love to abide there as a holy, healing medicine.

Pray:

   2) that the lies you accepted about yourself be brought to death on the cross and that you be set free to see and embrace yourself as Jesus does.

Pray:

   3) in repentance for any condemning judgments you made, especially against your parents. Make choices to forgive, and expect Jesus to make those choices become a reality.

Pray:

   4) renouncing your practiced expectations. Ask for a new and right spirit within.

Pray:

   5) that the Lord will melt the walls of your heart and cause your fleshly defenses to crumble so you may be protected by His breastplate and shield as you step forward into vulnerability and unfamiliar territory.

Pray:

   6) taking authority over the inner vows you have made, breaking their influence over you.

Pray:

7) that the old messages which misrepresented the desires of your heart and blocked God's plan for you be obliterated — and that new messages of blessing and invitation issue from you under the direction of the Holy Spirit.

8) WALK IN YOUR PRAYERS.

Family Support Groups

There are many kinds of small group structures which can provide friendship and nurture for singles. Sometimes the richest quality of experience happens in a Christian group which is made up of many combinations — the old and the young, male and female, couples and singles.

In such a group, the single person can enjoy the sense of family around her (or him). If she did not receive nurture in her own natural family, it is as available to her as she is willing and able to receive. If she was wounded by her natural family, she now has a chance to be healed through prayer and to enjoy a new experience with those who have been equipped to model healthy relationships, to carry her in their hearts, and to love her to life. Her Christian family is now in place to complement and encourage her. They can, with unconditional love, build into her a Christian identity and self-esteem she needs in order to become all that she can be.

If she has children, there are likely to be father models and marriage models within the group from whom the children can drink and learn. Throughout the Bible there is a powerful call to the Church to plead for and provide for the widows and the orphans.

The Blessings and Perils of Singles' Groups

Ideally, singles' groups should offer opportunities for people to gather to meet people and experience refreshing and supportive fellowship which takes the edge off of loneliness. They should provide a measure of security in belonging, and offer healing ministry to those who seek it.

If singles' groups create a wholesome environment of fun and adventure, meaningful conversation, recreation, and stimulating corporate study and/or service projects, lasting relationships will have an opportunity to develop.

All groups, single or otherwise, need some sort of focus outside of themselves, else they can easily become ingrown, self-seeking or problem-centered — depending on the security, self-esteem and stability of those who are a part of them.

John and I have seen some very healthy singles' groups. We have had the privilege of participating in a number of beautiful weddings and we have watched the positive growth of marriages birthed in such groups. But we have also listened to many tales of disappointment and disillusionment:

"Aren't there any decent men out there? I met a fellow at the singles group at my church. I thought

I might really get interested in him. But he wanted to take me to bed on our first date!"

Almost as often we have heard the same sort of comments from men:

"Aren't there any old-fashioned, virtuous women left in the world? I took a girl out to dinner and a show and she treated me like some sort of weirdo when I didn't make a pass at her!"

"I went to a Christian singles' group hoping to *meet* a nice girl who had the makings of a good wife. But it turned out to be a *meat market!*"

(The term "meat market" may sound offensive to some readers. But we have to face reality and recognize that this is an expression commonly used to describe what is happening too often in our culture today.)

A large church in which my husband and I have ministered a number times was keenly aware of the problems, needs and confusions growing in their membership. Throughout the year they presented several excellent series of studies concerning family, vocations, personal Christian identity, and healthy relationships. Then they offered a course which emphasized sexuality.

As a part of their advertising they developed a slogan which made it clear that their group did not exist for the purpose of shopping for sexual partners. "We are not a MEAT market! Come to MEET new friends!"

While one of our sons was attending seminary he decided to go to a singles' group in a very large, well-known church in the area. The church had a reputation for being enthusiastically alive, and he was seeking the refreshing fellowship of friends who might not be so enmeshed in the intensity of academic study as were his fellow students. But his hopeful expectations were quickly disappointed. He shared his disillusionment with us.

"They come every Sunday, lift their hands to worship the Lord with song and praise, clap vigorously to applaud all that God has done — and then go out to fornicate all week! With little or no conscience!"

The parents of a young woman who attended the singles group of one of the greatest churches in America shared with us their grief and concern that their daughter had been propositioned twelve times after the meeting on her way across the parking lot!

I do not mean to paint a black and critical picture of singles' groups. On the contrary, as I stated earlier, we have seen much good fruit produced in them. The likelihood of a girl being propositioned on a college campus, at a party, or at a bar would be infinitely greater than at a church-related singles group. We have prayed with hundreds of young men and women who are earnestly searching for wholesome and lasting relationships, to find one another somewhere in the midst of the wilderness of our modern culture.

We simply have to recognize that we live in a world where the absoluteness of God's law has been eroded from the culture and where illicit sex has been incessantly portrayed as the desirable norm in movies and literature. Numerous high school, and even some junior high young people have told us that they are ridiculed by many of their peers if they have not had sexual experience.

The older generation has difficulty understanding the tremendous pressures under which our young people live. We have trained our young people to be highly competent in the arts and sciences, and have sadly neglected to train them adequately in the skills of Christian marriage and family relationships.

Too often Christians have imposed sexual taboos on our children and teenagers with no real communication concerning the blessed holiness of marital sex. The power of a dictatorial "no-no" in the life of a teenager who is in the process of individuating from her/his parents is the force to drive her/him into rebellion, and thus into extreme vulnerability to peer pressure.

If the world continues to boldly and skillfully deliver the delusive message that sex in whatever circumstance or relationship is to be desired and sought after, and no one tells our young people about the sexual glory the Lord designed for them within godly parameters, how can our young people know the truth? How can they understand that they are exchanging their birthright for a miserable and sickening mess of pottage?

Secular sex education has made attempts to arm students with information for the protection of their physical well-being. But God is calling Christians to understand and speak clearly concerning the relationship between the sexuality and spirituality of every person, especially as we are equipped or disequipped to enter into real intimacy.

God Himself invented sex.
If it was His idea, why are we having such problems?

People don't understand the relationship of body and spirit. It is impossible for one person to touch another only physically. Our personal spirit is not poured into our body like water into a container. Our personal spirit gives life to our body (James 2:26) and flows through all its cells. Therefore, when we touch another, our spirit is also involved.

> Or do you not know that the one who joins himself to a harlot *is one body with her? 'THE TWO WILL BECOME ONE FLESH.'* But the one who joins himself to the Lord is one spirit with Him. Flee immorality. Every other sin that a man commits is outside the body, but the immoral man sins against his own body. Or do you not know that your body is a temple of the Holy Spirit who is in you, whom you have from God, and that you are not your own? For you have been bought with a price: therefore glorify God in your body." (1 Cor. 6:16-20)

God has created husbands and wives to become one flesh in holy covenant union (Gen. 2:24, Eph. :31). He has so built a man that in union with his wife, his spirit reaches out to enfold, protect, and nurture her. A woman is built to embrace and nurture her husband.

When two become flesh in unholy union, their spirits reach out to latch on because that is what they were created to do. Adulterers and fornicators meet in sinful perversion of God's intent. They have not been given His permission and blessing in marriage, and cannot complete one another in holiness. Their union tells lies one to the other about who they are, and causes them to carry confusion within them from their coming together.

If a person has lain with many partners, his/her spirit's focus and energies are scattered, seeking the many with whom he/she was joined; and it has become impossible to bond with only one. Therefore there is a need, wherever there has been an unholy union, or worse, a molestation, to pray that the Lord himself will wield His sword of truth to separate the personal spirit of the one from the other, so that each can be free to be wholly given and present to his or her own mate.

Following the guidance of the Holy Spirit, we have also prayed, directing the personal spirit in the name of Jesus to forget the union. The mind will never forget — for humility and compassion's sake — but the spirit needs to be set free to forget the latching on. Many for whom we have prayed in this way have exclaimed, "I feel so *together*. I didn't realize how scattered I was!"

Many singles who have been sexually active before marriage expect to be better equipped by experience to be great lovers. As a counselor I can tell you that it works in just the opposite way. When they marry, they have countless problems.

They have forfeited the discovery of the wonder of physical intimacy in the light of God's blessing, the unspoiled treasure of privateness, the sharing with one another what is theirs and theirs alone.

They are severely crippled in their ability to bond. Until repentance has happened and the Lord sets their spirits free, they go to bed dragging with them shadows of every other sexual encounter they have had.

Perhaps the most damaging is that they have already identified sexual intercourse as physical titillation at best. However good that may have seemed, it *cannot* have carried with it the glory God intends for a man and his wife to share.

As a couple come together in union, *meeting and embracing one another* body to body, heart to heart, mind to mind, spirit to spirit in complete intimacy, the Holy Spirit moves to sing through each of them into the other — first into their personal spirits, then through their spirits into every cell of their individual bodies, and on into the other as an exhilarative gift and a holy blessing of love. *The Holy Spirit will not sing in immoral places!*

God wants us to enjoy sex. His moral laws are guidelines for our protection so that we don't corrupt, distort, and lose His good gifts.

> Drink water from your own cistern, and fresh water from your own well. Should your springs be dispersed abroad, streams of water in the streets? Let them be yours alone, and not for strangers with

you. Let your fountain be blessed, and *rejoice in the wife of your youth. As a loving hind and a graceful doe, let her breasts satisfy you at all times; be exhilarated always with her love.* For why should you, my son, be exhilarated with an adulteress, and embrace the bosom of a foreigner? For the ways of a man are before the eyes of the Lord, and He watches all his paths. His own iniquities will capture the wicked, and he will be held with the cords of his sin. He will die for lack of instruction, and in the greatness of his folly he will go astray. (Prov. 5:15, *italics mine*)

It's not easy being single. In today's society your hormones turn on a number of years before you find your mate. Unfortunately for many, when their hormones turn on, their brains fall out, and they follow passion into a mess of confusion and hurt. As I have already explained, there is a way back to sanity and holiness through the forgiveness and the healing power of Jesus. But grace is never cheap, either for the Lord or for you.

I would make several very practical suggestions:

1. Set some boundaries for yourself which you will not cross. How far will you go with one who is not your husband? When passions *begin* to rise — STOP. The road of passion leads to covenant relationship. Covenant is forever.

2. Don't fall for anyone's line:

"If you love me you will..." — If he really loves you he will wait, respecting you. If you "do" and he "doesn't" you've hit the wall at the end of a dead end street — hard!

"I feel like we're already married in spirit." — Great. But wait until the rest of you gets married, and don't set too long an engagement period.

3. God may very well have the right person out there for you. Pray blessing for him to come, discernment to recognize him when he arrives. Keep yourself clean for his sake. Don't let any shopper handle the merchandise until he has signed the papers.

My husband remembers getting hot and bothered as a kid in high school. He remembers cooling down with the thought, "But she is not mine. I can't take what will someday rightfully belong to another."

4. Even when you're sure you've found the right one, be determined not to jump the gun and by it dull the excitement and intrigue of your honeymoon. A young lady I know has been living with her boyfriend for a year already. They're planning a big wedding — I wish them well — but where are the surprises?

Our son Tim and his wife found a long engagement to be a difficult test of resolve and endurance. They dated as much as they could in the company of friends. They watched TV and talked in the school lounge. If the lounge was crowded and they went to Victoria's room, they left her door open.

When helpful friends would go by and close the door for them, they would open it again. And they made it to the altar with an amazing amount of innocence still intact. If you should ask them, "Was it worth it?", their answer is "Yeah!" Today, more in love than ever, they have a solid marriage and three beautiful children.

5. Stay out of parked cars and other dark corners. In case you hadn't noticed, we girls can do quite a bit of long-term hugging without going overboard; guys are not made that way. Is "date-rape" a common issue today partly because we haven't done our biology homework? Try bicycling, tennis, raquetball . . . John and I have been happily (and still romantically) married for over forty years. We were friends before we were lovers.

6. If nothing seems to be happening for you, don't fantasize or dwell on your frustrations or unfulfilled dreams. Focus outward. Meet people. Make friends by being one, invest yourself in some sort of support group. Take hold of every healthy opportunity for life that comes your way (remembering that this is not anything like "any port in a storm." God wants you to have His best.)

7. Pray for a *gift* of celibacy (temporary, of course). It's a viable solution, and a good gift. Today's alternatives

may be AIDS or atrophy. Think about it. Without a gift of celibacy, many go on to follow desire and temptation into illicit sex, and thus, AIDS may be the result. Some who strive to be celibate without the gift, either lose their ability to function or fear that they will.

9
Divorce, and God's Mercy

"Be merciful, just as your Father is merciful" (Luke 6:36)

Divorce is not the unforgivable sin. If it were, then a possible way out of a miserable marriage might be to murder your spouse! A wife could be forgiven the sin of murder, and go on with her life in the more acceptable state of widowhood. In that role she would be legally free to marry, and someday someone might even ask her to give her testimony at a Christian ladies' luncheon.

I am in no way making light of the seriousness of marriage vows nor of the absoluteness of God's law. God hates divorce (Mal. 2:16). But He does not hate the divorcee! He hates the pain and anguish that not only the divorcee, but all the family and close friends have to walk through! He knows what devastating pain it is because He himself has borne our grief and carried our sorrows (Isa. 53:4).

The other half of Malachi 2:16 goes on to say, "and him who covers his garment with wrong." Granted, there are many who have made no real effort to reconcile their troubled marriage, and then go from one relationship to another without ever coming to awareness or repentance for sinful and dysfunctional areas of their own hearts.

Our modern-day culture has made it easy to do that by desensitising people to the grief their self-centered actions bring to others, especially their children, and to God. "They cover their garments with wrong" can be verbalized according to the strongholds of the day: "I deserve some happiness." "He/she doesn't understand me." My children would be better off without me." "I need to be free so I can find out who I am."

But I plead the question, "Is such self-centered flippancy the sin of *all* who have gone through divorce?" Absolutely not! And even if it were, would that excuse Christians who cover their own garments with wrong in the form of condemning judgment projected upon divorced people?

Jesus himself called us to "Be merciful, just as your Father is merciful." Immediately He went on to add, "And do not judge and you will not be judged; and do not condemn, and you will not be condemned; pardon, and you will be pardoned" (Luke 6:36,37). And yet divorced people are made to feel like outcasts or second class citizens in many congregations, rather than receiving much-needed ministry from those whom God has designed and called to be His healing body.

The death of a marriage usually carries with it much the same grief one experiences in the loss of a loved one by physical death. But divorce can be even more devastating because of feelings of failure, rejection, and betrayal.

Even though there is sometimes a tremendous sense of relief to be out of a situation where rancor and abuse have repeatedly caused hearts to bleed uncontrollably, a multi-residue of emotional sicknesses is likely to remain:

1. I made a bad choice. Can I trust my judgment again? Why didn't I recognize the danger signals while I might still have done something about them?

2. I couldn't live with him. But how will I live without him? I can't face being alone for the rest of my life.

3. I'm vulnerable and I'm afraid of my own neediness. I'm smart enough to know that "any-port-in-a-storm" would spell trouble for me, but I don't really know what I'd do if some smooth operator showed up with warm persuasion and caught me in a weak moment.

4. What do I do with my sexual drive? Sometimes I feel lustful — not toward anyone in particular. My feelings are just there. I feel guilty for having them, but I don't know what to do with them, and I feel dirty. Sometimes I'm afraid people can see inside of me and I want to hide.

5. Maybe I *should* hide. My husband didn't like me. Maybe there *is* something wrong with me. I surely don't feel attractive.

6. Sometimes I wish I could just die and go to heaven. I don't feel like I belong here. Even

some of our old *close* friends get uptight when I'm around — as if I were a potential husband-snatcher. Or they avoid me, as if hanging around would force them to take sides.

7. The most important thing: What have I done to my children? Can I ever make it up to them? What if they hate me for not making a safe nest for them? I hope they don't think it's their fault!

8. How can I take care of my kids? Child support won't be enough to supplement what I can make. Will we have to move? What if my car breaks down? What if something happens to me? What will the kids do?

9. My children need a father. Is it all right for me to remarry? What does the Bible say? What does the church say? What would people think of me? The questions go on, ad infinitum — to the point of exhaustion. Who can sleep restfully?

What Does the Bible Say About Divorce?

I believe we need to address this question from within the context of the Eastern culture in which the Bible was written, lest we relate only to legalisms and miss elements of God's purpose for the Law. The Law was given primarily to protect you, not to punish you!

For centuries it has been possible for a husband in Arab lands to divorce his wife by a spoken word. The wife thus divorced is entitled to all her wearing apparel, and the husband cannot take from her anything she has upon her own person. For this reason, coins on the headgear, and rings and necklaces, became important in the hour of the divorced woman's great need. This is one reason why there is so much interest in the bride's personal adornment in Eastern countries. Such customs of divorce were no doubt prevalent in Gentile lands in Old Testament times. It was for this reason that the law of Moses limited the power of the husband to divorce his wife, by requiring that he must give her a *written* bill of divorcement (Deut. 24:1). Thus the Jewish custom of divorce was superior to the Arabic.

It is important to remember that the sin of adultery did not have anything to do with the matter of divorce under Jewish law. That sin was punishable by death (Lev. 20:10; Deut. 22:22), and that by stoning. If a husband found any unseemly thing in his wife, he could give her a written bill of divorcement, which made it possible for her to marry another man (Deut. 24:2). A man guilty of unfaithfulness was considered to be a criminal only in that he had invaded the rights of another man. A woman was not allowed to divorce her husband. The prophet Malachi taught that God hated "putting away," and condemned severely any man who dealt treacherously with the wife of his covenant (Mal. 2:14-16). Such was the attitude of the Hebrew people on the subject of divorce. The

Lord Jesus swept away all grounds for divorce under the Law, and made unfaithfulness the lone grounds for divorce under the Christian dispensation (Matt. 5:31,32). — Fred H. Wight, *Manners and Customs of Bible Lands,* Moody Press, 1989, p. 125

Notice the progression in favor of protecting women from abusive whims of men who would treat them simply as chattel and put them away for anything which, in the eyes of a displeased husband, could be said to appear to be "unseemly."

Jesus' said, in Matthew 19:9, "And I say to you, whoever divorces his wife, *except for immorality* (Greek *moixeuo,* which means 'adultery'), and marries another woman commits adultery' " (italics mine). The same message was given in Matthew 5:31,32, with the added comment that if the man divorces his wife for any reason other than unchastity, he *makes* her commit adultery, and whoever marries a divorced woman commits adultery.

Even the disciples, steeped in traditional ways of thinking, objected to the new restriction on men. "The disciples said to Him, 'If the relationship of the man with his wife is like this, it is better not to marry' " (Matt. 19:10).

What more powerful deterrent could be given to prevent a woman from becoming the victim of a husband who could not (largely because of cultural tradition) fully see her as a person, but more like a thing to serve his pleasure! If she were put away, she and her family would carry the shame of it. And though she would be obliged to remarry, she could not then marry well, nor with honor.

As I wrote in Chapter Two, Jesus began to restore the relationship between men and women to God's original design. Paul continued in that track. Today in many countries of the world a woman is allowed to initiate divorce on the same grounds as her husband.

As men and women truly learn to walk in the Lord's Holy Spirit, there should be more and more ability to respect and cherish the unique person of the other. By the same token, there should be a great deal more reverence in the hearts of God's people for the eternal laws of God. But reverence for God's law is worlds away from legalism!

The letter of the law kills.

We must understand that the same God who gave us the Law is also He who:

...Made us adequate as servants of a new covenant, not of the letter, but of the Spirit, for the letter kills, but the Spirit gives life (2 Cor. 3:6).

Our Lord is by nature a God of mercy.

But God, being rich in mercy, because of His great love with which He loved us, even when we were dead in our transgressions, made us alive together with Christ (by grace you have been saved)..."

(Eph. 2:4)

214   HEALING WOMEN'S EMOTIONS

God does not owe us an explanation for His acts of mercy:

. . . I will have mercy on whom I have mercy, and I will have compassion on whom I have compassion.   (Rom. 9:15)

God's people are called to express His mercy:

Be merciful, just as your Father is merciful.
(Luke 6:36)

For judgment will be merciless to one who has shown no mercy; mercy triumphs over judgment.
(James 2:13)

If we can partake of the merciful heart of our Lord, then we will have no trouble accepting what Paul says:

For the unbelieving husband is sanctified through his wife, and the unbelieving wife is sanctified through her believing husband; for otherwise your children are unclean, but now they are holy. *Yet if the unbelieving one leaves, let him leave; the brother or the sister is not under bondage in such cases, but God has called us to peace.* For how do you know, O wife, whether you will save your husband? Or how do you know, O husband, whether you will save your wife? Only, *as the Lord has assigned to each one, as God has called each, in this manner let him walk.* And thus I direct in all the churches.

(1 Cor. 7:14-17, italics mine)

How can we distinguish "believing" from "unbelieving"?

Belief certainly involves more than what we profess with our lips. Jesus said, "THIS PEOPLE HONORS ME WITH THEIR LIPS, BUT THEIR HEART IS FAR FROM ME" (Matt. 15:8, Mark 7:6).

A number of years ago a man and his wife came to us for counseling. Both professed to be Christians, but their marriage was in deep trouble. As we listened to the two of them, it became more and more obvious that she was vigorously hugging all the righteousness to herself and persistently attacking him, not only directly, but throughout the community wherever anyone would give her audience. He acknowledged his sins and repented; she owned none.

During our devotional time the Holy Spirit led John and me to a Scripture that leapt off the page to us:

There is a kind who is pure in his own eyes, yet is not washed from his filthiness. There is a kind — oh how lofty are his eyes! And his eyelids are raised in arrogance. There is a kind of man whose teeth are like swords, and his jawteeth like knives, to devour the afflicted from the earth, and the needy from among men.　　(Prov. 30:12-14)

We exclaimed almost simultaneously, "That's it! There she is! Just change the pronouns — *her* eyes, *her* eyelids, *woman* whose teeth!"

Her husband was not only bleeding from her constant ripping and tearing. He was dying emotionally and spiritually, and his physical health was beginning to crumble. But he was determined to pursue reconciliation. We did all we could to help them both, but she would have none of it.

Finally he divorced her, and later married a woman who knows how to nurture his heart. The Lord, in His mercy, has abundantly blessed their relationship, finances, health and the ministry into which He has called them.

What about his ex-wife? She is still in the community doing what she has always done. Romans 3 describes her behavior fairly well:

THEIR THROAT IS AN OPEN GRAVE, WITH THEIR TONGUES THEY KEEP DECEIVING, THE POISON OF ASPS IS UNDER THEIR LIPS; WHOSE MOUTH IS FULL OF CURSING AND BITTERNESS; THEIR FEET ARE SWIFT TO SHED BLOOD, DESTRUCTION AND MISERY ARE IN THEIR PATHS, AND THE PATH OF PEACE HAVE THEY NOT KNOWN. THERE IS NO FEAR OF GOD BEFORE THEIR EYES.(Rom. 3:13-18)

Yet to this day she is convinced that she has been the only righteous one in their entire history, and that God will bring her husband back to her!

Would it have been God's first will to restore this marriage? Of course. But in a case such as this, where one partner relentlessly and unrepentantly persists in aggressive, destructive behavior which literally destroys the life of the other, reconciliation may be rendered impossible. God will not violate anyone's free will. God may, however, express His mercy, and deliver the exhausted but sincerely repenting, forgiving and foreign wounded one from the war zone.

Did the wedding ever become a marriage?

Jesus quotes from Genesis 2:24, saying, "FOR THIS CAUSE A MAN SHALL LEAVE HIS FATHER AND MOTHER, AND SHALL CLEAVE TO HIS WIFE; AND THE TWO SHALL BECOME ONE FLESH." Suppose that cleaving has never been accomplished because the prerequisite of leaving has never happened? Leaving necessarily precedes cleaving.

Has the husband cut free from the bondage of parental allegiances that are no longer appropriate? Vows may have been mouthed in the wedding ceremony, but has a one-flesh marriage become reality? Or is he now in a spiritually adulterous relationship with his parents, while blindly and stubbornly defending his position?

I have listened to the woeful tales of a number of women who have lived for years with "husbands" who either had never had sexual relations with their wives, or they did so only for a short time after the wedding, and then fled from intimacy altogether.

These women had pursued previous counseling for themselves, but their "mates" stubbornly refused to acknowledge that there was a problem. The women were deeply wounded because they bore the title of "Mrs." but in reality were only cooks, housekeepers, hostesses, dinner companions, laundresses. They felt belittled, rejected, and used, yet legally bound in what had never been a marriage.

What were their stated reasons for remaining in such a relationship? "Because I am afraid of what he might do." "Because he is well thought of in our town and I'm afraid of what people might think of me." "Because my church teaches against divorce and I'd be condemned." "Because I'm afraid I might lose my salvation."

Jesus said, "What therefore God has joined together, let no man separate (Matt. 19:6)." Did God join anyone *together* in such cases? Some words were said which were formal entrance into what didn't even begin to be the kind of relationship God has in mind for a man and a woman. The Lord in His wisdom may know that there is no hope for change.

I strongly believe that God himself can, and surely *may* choose, in His mercy, to put asunder what men and women in their naivete or foolishness have only thought to put together. I would further suggest that when repentance is real, and forgiveness has been given by the Lord, He may also grant His grace for new beginnings.

The words of the Psalmist have settled as a comforting balm into countless broken hearts:

Remember, O LORD, Thy compassion
   and Thy lovingkindnesses,
      For they have been from of old.
Do not remember the sins of my youth
   or my transgressions;
According to Thy lovingkindness remember Thou
me,
For Thy goodness sake, O LORD. (Ps. 25:6,7)

Sometimes very young girls leave home in rebellion, fleeing in hurt and fear and confusion. They have no idea what might wait for them out there in the world, but the excruciatingly familiar abuse they have suffered at home can no longer be tolerated. They run . . . . . and run . . . . . and run . . . . . to exhaustion and futility.

Where can a thirteen-year-old find work? Where can a penniless thirteen-year-old obtain something to eat and a place to sleep? She is convinced that nothing could be as bad as what she has left behind. Returning home is unthinkable. But she is hungry, and cold, and very much alone.

What defense does she have against the pimps? The drug dealers? Any other kind of opportunist? She has no developed discernment to identify and reject trouble in unfamiliar forms, no maturity to enable her to project into the future and weigh the possible results of her decisions.

Her emotions are in chaos. She is easy prey for anyone offering any kind of tangible comfort. If she finds a man who seems to make reasonable promises to care for her, she may attach herself to him out of need; she may even marry him at some point. Suppose then that she later discovers she has latched onto more of a nightmare than the one she ran from in the first place. Would our loving and compassionate God hold her to that covenant forever?

Jeannie was thirteen when she left the nightmare she had lived in at home to follow a dream and a promise.

Her mother had "gone away" when her daughter was only two; Jeanie could hardly remember, and no one would talk about what had happened. Her father was an often violent, falling-down-drunk. Her brothers were angry and abusive with no one to stop them.

Occasionally, when things became more than she could bear, she'd manage to slip away and take a long walk around the neighborhood, though she knew she was sure to be punished when she returned. Sometimes she dreamed about living in someone else's home.

She had noticed other children playing happily in their yards who would sometimes be called in for cookies or other treats. She never knew what would happen when a member of her family opened the back door to call her name. She wished she had a friend she could talk to.

There was a man several blocks away who noticed the sad little girl as she walked by his house. He would often stop what he was doing to talk to her. Sometimes he would ask her to sit on his front porch to rest. He was so understanding and compassionate that for a little while she didn't feel so alone and afraid. He seemed to be everything her father wasn't. Her visits became more and more frequent, and Jeanie began to pour out her heart to him.

One day the kind man gave her an invitation that she felt could only have come out of her fondest dreams. He had been given a new job and would be moving very soon to another city — to a house even nicer than the one he was living in now. Would she like to go with him? He was alone and she would be his family, and he would take very good care of her.

Jeanie followed her dream. No one from home either prevented or pursued her. At first it was exciting. And then reality began to hit her. The kind man was not at all interested in being the father she had never had! Once again she was an object of abuse, and soon she was a mother. But she had no idea of what it meant to be either wife or mother. Babies kept appearing until there were five. There was never a wedding, but she stayed with him in a common-law situation for more than eighteen years.

During those years her "husband" began to drink more and more. He became increasingly abusive and violent just as her father had been. She became fearful for her two daughters who remained at home. Seeking help through the church, she developed a relationship with the Lord, and over a period of time gained enough inner strength and self-esteem to stand up and say "no" to her common-law husband.

She left him, found a minimum-wage job, studied to earn her GED, and did a creditable job of struggling to provide a home for her girls. After a time she was forced to seek welfare aid. There was never enough money to cover all their physical needs, but there seemed to be much more safety in poverty than she had known in the relationship from which she had fled.

Later Jeanie (and her girls) developed a love relationship with a man who asked her to marry him. After a time of testing and Christian counsel, she did. But he was a divorced man. The legalists, sharks in her church, circled to attack, unconcerned about her history of abuse, not seeking or wanting knowledge of the circumstances out of which either had come.

I believe that Jesus is still speaking the same words to the Pharisees as He did 2000 years ago, "But go and learn what this means, 'I DESIRE COMPASSION AND NOT SACRIFICE,' for I did not come to call the righteous, but sinners" (Matt. 9:13).

Many other varieties of situations call for compassion:

"I thought I knew my husband when I married him. We have two beautiful children. Now I've discovered that all this time he has been secretly engaging in homosexual relationships. I feel betrayed and dirty. I'm afraid for my sons. I love him, but he refuses help. I can't stay with him, but I'm afraid to face life alone. My children need a father. Can I marry again?"

"I was a rebellious teen when I married, and my husband and I were both heavily into the drug scene. I got out, but he didn't. He says he won't. He wants me back, but I can't return to that life-

style or the crowd he's still running with. I'm a
Christian now. My husband thinks I'm crazy.
Some people tell me I have to go back to him. But
I hate everything he stands for. Going back would
be like a death sentence. I'm still young. I've truly
repented for my sins. I must be born again for
something. I don't have any particular guy in
mind, but at least I would like to have a chance
for a good wholesome life with someone — a
home and kids. I'm not getting any younger."

If we are going to call ourselves Christians we must
be careful to meet each individual as a person for whom
Christ died. It is fitting to realize that were it not for
the grace of God in our lives, we might well be
suffering even as they are. We must not allow ourselves
to form hard opinions concerning them from what
appears on the surface of their lives. If we live and pray
in Jesus' name we can never judge another with
condemnation. We must not fall into the pharisaical
error of making blanket statements concerning people
who have suffered the devastating pain of divorce.

On the other hand, I am not going to make blanket
proclamations of mercy which would preclude anyone's
own necessary soul-searching. "Only, as the Lord has
assigned to each one, as God has called each, in this
manner let him walk. And thus I direct in all the
churches" (1 Cor. 7:14-17).

I do warn everyone not take the laws of God lightly;
He holds us accountable. I urge all to pray for wisdom,

discernment and trust to recognize and accept God's best will.

If your husband has rejected you for another woman, or simply for irreconcilable differences, don't allow yourself to become caught in the bondage of super-intensive trying-by-whatever-means to get him back. Perhaps the Holy Spirit has told you to pray diligently for reconciliation. Respond obediently. Contest his action — especially if you have children. He may not even begin to know his own mind. But I caution you against setting all your hope on your husband's return as though your very life depended on it. Some women have persisted in this direction to the point of idolatry and insufferable manipulation.

Some women have even continued to battle in prayer though the divorced husband has long ago remarried and fathered a child or two by his new wife. Now there are innocent young children to consider. Issues become very complicated, and there is no cleanly moral way out, even though the letter of the Law might declare you the righteous one.

Be assured that whether your marriage is restored at some future date or not, the Lord will never abandon you as a person. He has a perfect plan and a meaningful purpose for you which He never forgets.

You may not yet know what it is, "But seek first His kingdom and His righteousness; and all these things shall be added to you" (Matt. 6:33). "Things" in this Scripture refers specifically to food, drink, clothing — material provisions about which we are instructed not to be anxious. I believe that godly supply for emotional and spiritual needs also attends our seeking after His kingdom and His righteousness.

I implore you not to try to be your own counselor. You are not in a position to have clear, unbiased perspectives concerning your own problems. Pray to find someone who will draw your thoughts out, who will listen with a compassionate ear, discuss and advise without controlling, and pray with you about all your issues.

It is important for you to find out what are the possible roots of dysfunction in yourself that may have contributed to the breakdown of your marriage and/or the prevention of its healing. You need to discover what factors operating in you may have caused you to be blind so that you chose wrongly.

If you continue to see with unchanged eyes, you could possibly repeat the same mistakes. The Lord, through His cross, wants to set you free from the past and cause you to grow into all He created you to be, including ability to participate fully in wholesome healthy relationships — perhaps later on with another man.

Look for a church which has a small support group structure in which you can develop a sense of belonging to a family. Give yourself opportunity to make new friends who will love you unconditionally, encourage and nurture you, advise and confront you with no condemnation, and provide for you when you have special needs. Enter that structure also with a determination to give yourself to serve others.

Know that God himself loves you unconditionally and eternally. You don't have to deserve or earn His love, and you can't lose it. Even His discipline is for your good.

He disciplines us for our good, that we may share His holiness. All discipline for the moment seems not to be joyful, but sorrowful; yet to those who have been trained by it, afterwards it yields the peaceful fruit of righteousness. Therefore strengthen the hands that are weak and the knees that are feeble, and make straight paths for your feet, so that the *limb* which is lame may not be put out of joint, but rather be healed.(Heb. 12:10-13)

The Lord's desire is not to punish you for your mistakes, but rather to discipline you in love so you don't unwittingly repeat those same errors. His desire is to redeem your mistakes and restore you to wholeness.

What about the questions (listed at the beginning of this chapter) that plague you?

1. You made a bad choice. Can you trust your judgment again? God will not only forgive your mistakes; He is able to redeem them. You can trust His ability to purify and transform your judgment. But He needs your invitation and cooperation.

2. You can't face being alone for the rest of your life? Don't be in a hurry to fill the void. God's arms are the only safe ones to rush into. When the news of your

divorce becomes public, the predators will try to close in on you. Some know they are taking advantage of your vulnerability and will do it anyway without conscience. Others are seeking solace and/or affirmation for themselves. They will unwittingly do it at your expense, pressuring you into sexual relationships, though they may have convinced themselves they only want to help you. Don't jeopardize what God may have planned for your future by grabbing something cheap to comfort you in your present moment of pain. Such comfort does away with your pain like poison gas.

3. You are afraid of your own neediness? Hallelujah! Tell God about it. Talk with a trusted friend.

4. What do you do with your sexual drive? Don't be ashamed of it. You are alive. You are also single now. Read chapter six about sex and singles. Sex in the aftermath of a divorce can be one of the most confusing, defiling and eventually humiliating experiences of your life.

5. You feel unattractive? Your body is a temple of the Holy Spirit (1 Cor. 6:19). God's temple is beautiful. Pray to see yourself with His eyes.

6. Old friends are uncomfortable around you? Choose to forgive. Busy yourself with things you like to do. Make new friends. The old ones, if they are genuine, will come back eventually. Remember, they are hurting also, and just don't know what to do or say.

7. How can you minister to your children? Talk to them. They need to hear your divorce is not their fault. Ask their forgiveness for failures and fractures. You

don't have to say it is all your fault; it may not be. But they need to know that you as primary adult in their life are deeply sorry for their sake that you were not able to maintain a secure, two-parent family environment for them.

Assure them that you will never leave them. Share with them quality times which include recreation. Give them compliments and copious affection appropriate to their age level. Do not fail in the least of your promises to them.

If you are going to be late arriving home from work, call them and let them know about it. They need the security of knowing where you are and that you are concerned for them. Encourage them to talk about their feelings. Assure them that it is okay to be angry, to be afraid.

Teach them by your example constructive ways of handling emotions like anger and fear. Pray with them, honestly expressing feelings, calling for God's comfort and strength, and confirming His loving presence with you (whether you feel it or not). PLAY with them. Life is heavy now, and the atmosphere can be lightened for you and them if you can regularly do fun things together.

8. Pray for a good job, good health, and the humility to ask for help when you need it. You may have to make severe financial adjustments which require prioritizings you have never had to deal with before. But the children will find their security much more in your personal loving attention and nurture than in

material provisions. Don't sacrifice their emotional and spiritual welfare for a job that takes you too much away from them.

9. It is not of primary importance what people think of you. It is extremely important what God thinks of you. But He already knows you better than you know yourself and is able to judge the thoughts and intentions of your heart with merciful understanding.

For we do not have a high priest who cannot sympathize with our weaknesses, but one who has been tempted in all things as we are, yet without sin. Let us therefore draw near with confidence to the throne of grace, that we may receive mercy and may find grace to help in time of need.(Heb. 4:15,16)

10
Mothers in Travail

Whenever a woman is in travail she has sorrow, because her hour has come; but when she gives birth to the child, she remembers the anguish no more, for joy that a child has been born into the world. (John 16:21)

My children, with whom I am again in labor until Christ be formed in you — (Gal. 4:19)

Motherhood has always been a tremendous privilege and responsibility which brings, I believe, joys and rewards that far outweigh possible difficulties and sorrows. A woman will never in any other circumstance have an opportunity to influence the life of another human being as profoundly as she does her own child.

She will not experience in any other situation the quality of satisfaction and deeply rooted exhilaration she receives as she watches her offspring grow to maturity with understanding and skills which surpass her own. Raising a child in the loving, life-giving nurture and discipline of the Lord is a sacred trust and an eternal work. There is no more important calling or anointing on the life of anyone, male or female.

However, in this present generation, emotional and spiritual responsibilities of parents have become

231

awesome and frightening because of the increasingly powerful seductive and defiling influences from our deteriorating culture which press in upon our children. While they are still babes, we can maintain some control over their environment, and they drink mostly from who we are.

Early parental problems have to do largely with diapers and toilet training, runny noses, bumps and bruises, eating, sleeping, cleaning up messes, and discovering what sort of discipline is appropriate to the little person who must learn freedom within safe and healthy parameters.

Frustrations begin to arise when that little one starts to push those boundaries and expresses resistance, sometimes emphatically, when mother/father vetoes unsupervised exploration of cupboards, drawers and toilet bowls. But mom and dad still find themselves often chuckling at the cuteness of their offspring.

They continue for a while to have confidence in their ability to carry him/her away from imminent danger. But when children begin, as they must, to experience life in the company of their peers, anxieties begin to well up in the hearts of parents who care. Will the deposit of love and training conscientious parents have put into their offspring be enough to enable them to resist the increasing force of negative outside influences?

Anxieties Have Increased With Our Changing Culture.

When my husband and I were raising our family, we

were very much concerned about the foul language our children heard from others in our neighborhood, but the potty-mouths were in the minority. Expression of profanity and filth were relatively limited and rather pale by today's standards.

Today such speech has become so commonplace that in the general populace few seem to be offended. Those who openly express their objections are often ridiculed as being "religious fanatics" or "Bible-thumpers."

Not too many years ago TV programs and movies were still subject to some rather strict censorship. Actors and actresses still wore pajamas in bedroom scenes, and intimate interludes were left largely to the imagination. Heroes were not yet applauded for sexual promiscuity. Now a family begins to enjoy what they think is a wholesome movie and suddenly find themselves viewing a pornographic episode which has little to do with the plot.

In previous generations, mischief was a normal part of growing up, but deliberately destructive vandalism was almost unheard of. For instance, it was a fairly common occurrence on a weekend for someone to wake up to find their lawn creatively toilet-papered by a group of partying teenagers, but school properties were not wantonly destroyed by eleven-and twelve-year-old delinquents.

School teachers were still given authority to discipline their students, even with a supervised paddling in many schools. Some parents may have complained, but in many homes parental discipline supported and reinforced school discipline.

Most children go through a period of fascination with lighting matches, which sometimes accidentally gets out of hand. Our son Johnny once set the corner of his bedspread on fire, and Tim started a more serious blaze in the basement of the parsonage where we lived, but both boys had the presence of mind to quench the flames before much damage was done. They also accepted the disciplinary consequences of their thoughtless adventures, and learned from the experiences.

I remember when my brothers and I became a bit too carried away with our game of "blazing" trails through the weeds in a vacant lot near our home. We had a wonderful time stomping out the fires as soon as we had set them, but mother noticed the undeniable evidence on our tennis shoes and hauled us to account verbally as well as on the seat of our britches. In those days, one did not hear of fires deliberately set by children for the sake of destruction.

Young boys used to play cops and robbers in backyards, alleys and vacant lots. It was only a game, and they would take turns being the "good guys," who were usually the winners. Today we read reports in our newspapers concerning young people who have brought real firearms to school, and children who have actually shot their playmates, teachers, or parents. Unmanageable pressures are increasing in the world today, and restraints are failing.

Very few young people in previous generations grew up without at least once trying cigarettes (or home-made facsimiles) and beer. By the time our children reached their teens, some drugs, mostly marijuana, were easily available, but not yet to grade school children. Now, young people can experiment just once with drugs like cocaine and become instantly addicted. We have to watch our street-corners and alleys carefully for pushers. And many children don't have to go outside their own homes for a ready supply of alcoholic beverages.

Fornication used to be commonly considered a sin. Recently James Dobson reported the following statistics:

> Today the National Center for Health Statistics reports that 29 percent of 15-year-olds are sexually active, and 81 percent of 19-year-olds!
>
> Seventy-two percent of 17-year-old boys are sexually active, as well as 88 percent of 19-year-olds.
>
> 1.5 million abortions occur each year, and the spread of 38 sexually transmitted diseases continues at epidemic proportions. A strain of gonorrhea has now appeared that is completely resistant to all known antibiotics.
>
> 27,000 cases of syphilis were reported in 1986 — and 44,000 in 1989.
>
> Twenty to 30 percent of college-age women are currently estimated to have genital herpes — a

disease from which they will suffer the rest of their lives.

— Dr. James C. Dobson, "The Second Great Civil War," *Focus on the Family,* November, 1990, p. 5

Now, since the stunning public revelation that a hero figure like Magic Johnson can become infected by the HIV virus, a great campaign has been launched to protect our young people by teaching them to use condoms as a means of ensuring "safe sex." I appreciate the intent to protect, but what a lie this communicates to our children!

Quite aside from the very real but frequently ignored, denied or minimized moral and sociological implications involved in promiscuity, there is a FACT which should be presented boldly and clearly to our young people. Condoms are *not* and never have been guarantors of safe sex. They fail in varieties of ways, and many people living today were conceived as a result of those failures.

Has the development and use of newer and more sophisticated means of birth control caused us to forget so completely that we can, with few or no pangs of conscience, communicate to our young people a false security?

As I write, I remind myself that this is supposed to be a book concerning the *healing* of women's emotions. Now I'm beginning to feel rather emotional myself as I identify with the grief and anxiety of countless mothers everywhere who see their children, especially teenagers, sucked into the stream of our polluted and seductive culture, and too often overcome by it.

We begin to experience a sense of helplessness to protect or retrieve our "babies" from the flood which threatens to destroy their lives. Don't despair. I *will* turn to a more positive and healing note. But first it is helpful to understand how we arrived in such a cultural predicament, and to become aware of popular "solutions" which are not likely to be adequate.

What Caused This Mess?

Too many children have been victims of father absence, largely because of wars which took fathers away from their homes and claimed the lives of many. When the wars ended, great numbers of those who returned were emotionally wounded and/or occupied with catching up with schooling and careers — to the extent that their children did not receive quality time and attention. Therefore, lacking adequate relationship and modeling for themselves, many men today have never known how to be nurturing and disciplining fathers. Some have abdicated their position unconsciously from ignorance, and others consciously from frustration and fear.

Respect for the absolute and eternal laws of God has been eroded. The pictures of God which children develop are significantly shaped and colored at the heart level by experiences with their natural fathers. If father did not cherish and protect them, how or why should Father God? If father rejected and abandoned them physically or emotionally, they will expect Father God to do the same. If father abused them, they will tend to see God as being harsh and unfair. If father was never there, children will have difficulty believing that God is real. If father was present physically but never showed any affection and never disciplined, his children will be unable to believe that God will hold them accountable in love.

Those who have been seriously wounded in any way by their natural fathers will be extremely vulnerable to humanistic voices advocating a kind of moral and spiritual anarchy that discounts the eternal laws of God and proclaims every person to be his or her own god. In this new system "my feelings" masquerade as truth, and "my needs" take priority over honesty and over the welfare of the whole family or other corporate groups.

Divorce rates have risen radically. Thousands of mothers (and an increasing number of fathers) are trying to raise children as single parents, usually under great stress. Even though they may be doing an admirable job, God never intended that sort of double duty, and did not equip them to be mother/father figures easily. Almost everywhere my husband and I travel, single parents are crying for help. Even though the Bible says again and again to care for the orphans, few churches or other organizations are structured to fulfill the needs of such a rapidly growing segment of our society.

People Are Reacting in Fear.

Many young married couples, wounded and intimidated by what they themselves have experienced, are making decisions not to give birth to children because they don't want the "terrible" responsibility of raising them in a world such as this.

Teenagers are having abortions with no conviction that they are committing murder for which they will eventually reap. And so-called "enlightened authorities" are persuading them with lies that there is really no moral issue involved.

Conversely, increasing numbers of teenagers and young women are giving birth to babies when they haven't the foggiest understanding of what it means to be a parent. They are at a naturally self-centered stage of their own development, and haven't the maturity to be able to sacrifice their own comfort or desire consistently for the sake of their babies.

Often teen-age pregnancy happens in the heat of passion with no thought that there may be a consequential price to pay. Some deliberately try to conceive, hoping this will bind a boyfriend to them. Some invite pregnancy because they have experienced rejection and want someone all their own to love.

They aren't aware that the motivating power for their affection is not first to bless the baby, but to comfort themselves. Unless there are family members to support these child-mothers until they grow up, they often neglect, abuse, and/or abandon their babies.

Many people who have chosen to raise families have substantial reasons to fear for their children, because they themselves lack the knowledge, experience, and wisdom necessary to provide the quality of love and discipline to build a sturdy foundation and secure family structure. They cannot model or communicate what they never received. Now, as problems arise, many are attempting too late, with anxiety and urgency, to seek help to equip themselves.

Others have become so pressured to maintain a certain standard of living, so consumed with career building, or so busy with personal interests outside the home, they have simply failed to spend quality time sharing themselves with their children.

Without realizing it, they have trained their sons and daughters from earliest years to look first or only outside the home environment for meaningful relationships, affirmation and answers to life's problems. Panic eventually hits, and they cry, "How could my children turn their backs on me when I have given them everything?" — Every *thing* yes, but *no real relationship with a primary person.*

Understanding Teens and Trusting God With Them.

Too few Christians have substantial enough faith in the overcoming power of Jesus Christ to trust God with the deposit of training and moral values they have seeded into the lives of their children. They tend to try too hard to control and protect their teenagers just at the time when it is appropriate to cut them free emotionally. Teens are necessarily in the process of *individuating* and establishing their *independence.*

They must, as they move into adulthood, say, "I am me. I am not you. I am my own person, and I have an opinion of my own." It is impossible for them to jump successfully from a child's position in the family where all decisions are made for them, to an adult position in which they are suddenly expected to manage their own lives.

So-called "model children" who, two weeks after they have left home to enroll in the university, suddenly flip out, are repeated testimony to that reality. The teen years need to be a time of transitional learning during which young people are considered to be adults, responsible before God for their own mistakes (a very biblical concept).

During this time a wise parent becomes a coach. He involves the teenager in the development of home rules for considerate living, and together they work out fair penalties for violations. Parents hold teenagers accountable for what has been agreed upon, and watch their own behavior so as not to model contrary values.

Teenagers desperately need parents who listen, who believe in them when they may be as yet insecure and unable to believe in themselves. They need their parents to trust them even when they can't be trusted. The home doors must be left open to the prodigal as parents watch prayerfully, so that when they come to themselves, their senses, as in Luke 15:17, they have a place to return to — loved ones who will receive them compassionately.

Teens are also involved in an essential natural process of accomplishing what we call *internalization.* They will and they must examine everything they have been taught, test many things, and come to decisions about what they will call their own. This is a large part of the reason they are so self-centered during this period or their lives. They are necessarily working on themselves.

Many parents don't understand what is going on, and even those who do, usually find teens difficult to live with patiently. But if anxious parents panic and push, treat them as children rather than as budding adults, or respond to questioning and testing with consistent criticism, teenagers perceive that parents have all the ground of righteousness occupied.

In order to be their own person they feel compelled to take an opposite stance, even though it may not be what they really want. In the midst of the battle which ensues, Christian parents then often drive teenagers beyond normal healthy individuation into *rebellion.* When rebellion has taken hold of young people, they become vulnerable to every prevailing stronghold in our culture.

I Am Not Saying That Parents Are to Blame for All of
the Rebellious Sins of Their Children.

Why? First, at some point in every person's life he/she

must take responsibility for his/her own responses. Second, in today's world we are surrounded by increasing confusion and wickedness. Much of it comes wrapped in attractive packages through television programing. Even if your children don't see it at home, they will be exposed to it to some extent in someone else's home.

A good deal of it is presented in the guise of enlightened knowledge and practical, scientific authority by godless ones who have infiltrated our educational system. In many places and ways, these humanists wield significant influence.

You can substitute with home schooling, but eventually your child will have to go out and associate with other people. Will his/her education be experientially adequate to prepare him/her to interact successfully with the people of the world? Will you send your child to Christian schools? A good Christian school may help, but many of the students in Christian schools are not yet Christian.

In fact, some of them are there because they have problems which the public schools cannot handle. Much of the world's confusion is passed on to our children by the other children with whom they associate. Children naturally want to be accepted among their peers, and they will be vulnerable to the attitudes and values of their friends. It is becoming increasingly difficult for a child to find a friend today who does not come from a dysfunctional family.

Some families are so dysfunctional they don't even recognize they have problems. Parents, no matter how hard they try, cannot altogether prevent their offspring from negative and harmful influences. They can, however, provide them with equipment to live with strength in the midst of a wicked and perverse generation, to stand and to be in but not of the world. Much of that equipment is built into a child by simple acts.

What Can a Mother Do to Build Strength into Her Child?

1. While your baby is in your womb, pray protection, blessing and welcome daily for him/her. Listen to melodious music. From conception, your baby has a sensitive personal spirit, or there would be no life in his/her little body at all (James 2:26). Your child in the womb has the capacity to experience, receive, and respond. If you faithfully voice the prayers, it is God's job to make something happen. Ask your husband to speak a father's blessing. Insofar as it is possible, stay out of tension-producing situations. Do not smoke or drink, or consume caffeine or take drugs. Eat a nourishing diet, get regular exercise, and plenty of rest.

2. Breastfeed your baby if at all possible. If you have trouble, consult La Leche League or WIC (Women-Infants-Children nutritional program) for helpful instruction. If for some reason beyond your control you must use a bottle, be sure always to cuddle the baby while feeding. You are not just pouring milk into your baby; you are pouring love.

3. Hold, and tenderly rock your baby. Talk and sing to him/her. Babies comprehend much more with their sensitive little spirits than they do with their minds. You cannot spoil a child with warm, clean, wholesome affectionate touch. By affection, copiously given, you *will* build in basic trust that he/she is chosen, precious, and he/she will settle into a secure sense of belonging.

4. Change baby's diapers — even the messy ones — with joy. Be delighted with the privilege! By this you teach him/her to accept, appreciate and respect natural body functions. Your attitude influences the baby's sexuality. Build into the baby quiet expectations to be comforted and not shamed.

5. Encourage your husband to participate in all of the above — except, of course, breast feeding. He is the first primary person to receive and carry the baby away from the familiar territory of mother. If his arms are strong and gentle, the baby will begin to develop positive anticipation of the world away from mother and security apart from her. It is the primary task of the father to draw the child forth into life. Proper nurture from a mother and a father give the baby courage to be, to adventure and risk, and to meet other people vulnerably, spirit to spirit. If your husband resists becoming involved, check your angers and give them to the Lord. God can handle your negative emotions; your baby would be wounded and confused by them.

6. Take time to play with your child. Laugh with him/her. Such a simple game as peek-a-boo teaches a baby that though you may disappear, you will surely return. Little children delight in repetition of experiences which write comfort and reassurance on their hearts.

7. Leave your child with a reliable baby-sitter once in a while. Your husband needs to have some romantic time just with you, and this also teaches your little one that though you may leave for a while, you have not abandoned him/her. However, do not leave your child with a sitter so much that he/she feels forsaken and begins to look to the sitter as the primary care-giver. Don't forfeit your privilege of parenthood. No one can adequately replace you. If it is absolutely necessary for you to work and leave your child in some sort of day care, be careful to spend consistent quality time with him/her at the end of each day. Tell your child, "I missed you! I am so glad to see you!" Tell him/her with words, hugs, and participation with him/her in activities which you both enjoy.

8. As your son or daughter develops, read stories, work and play together. Encourage, compliment, listen, teach with patience, give appropriate hugs and kisses. Let discipline be applied consistently with love, never with condemnation.

9. By your example teach your child to pray. God is compassionately interested in personal issues such as skinned knees, bruises, disappointments and hurt feelings. He understands our fears and does not ridicule our tears. Train your child to talk to the Lord simply and directly about problems as they arise. Our own children have done that for their children, because we did it for them.

One afternoon our daughter-in-law Victoria was searching diligently for a contact lens she had dropped. She had just purchased lenses and was becoming increasingly upset with the thought of having to spend money from their very tight budget to replace one so soon. Tears were beginning to well up when Rachel, barely three-years-old, noticed her mother's distress.

"Why are you crying, Mama?"

"Because I've looked everywhere and I can't find my contact lens."

Rachel instantly raised her little arm into the air and prayed confidently, "Jesus, find mama's lens, please."

Immediately Victoria saw her contact lens on the bathroom floor beneath her feet.

"Rachel — look! Jesus answered your prayer!"

"Uh huh," Rachel acknowledged matter-of-factly.

Rachel did what came naturally because faith and prayer had been modeled into her. Even at that tender age and in the face of the rising anxiety her mother was experiencing, she was able to express her trust in Jesus' ability and desire to help.

Share also your joys and gratitudes together, giving thanks to God for His loving presence, protection, and provision. *You are a living epistle. You represent God to your child.*

10. Pray protection for your children as they begin to venture into the neighborhood. Arm them with some common-sense understanding, but do not overprotect. How will they learn the meaning of comfort and healing if they are never allowed to stumble and fall? How will they learn the delightful refreshment of a warm bath if they are not allowed to get dirty? Hold them accountable for their mistakes with firm and fair discipline — for their good — not to make them behave so you can look good. Communicate the message, "I love you too much to let you get by with this." Never excommunicate them from your love. Be warmly available.

11. When your children become teenagers, remember what I wrote earlier in this chapter, and in prayer cut them totally free from you. In the flesh, we would emotionally bind our children to us so that they could not become their own persons with their own center of decision. Bite your tongue when tempted to give unsolicited advice. When they ask you for advice, tell them less than you would like to say. Give them opportunity to draw information from you. Listen to their opinions and try not to register too much shock or alarm, they may be only testing you. Hear them out.

12. Pray for the protection of your children at every level of their development. Especially when they are in their teens, stand with and for them in spiritual warfare against the forces of darkness in the world which would press in to threaten, seduce, attack, oppress, or push them in any way. Command those forces to stand back in the name of Jesus.

Then pray for your children that they be strengthened in their inner man, their own personal spirit, to make their own righteous decisions:

For this reason I bow my knees before the Father, from whom every family in heaven and on earth derives its name, that He would grant you, according to the riches of His glory, **to be strengthened with power through His Spirit in the inner man;** so that Christ may dwell in your hearts through faith; and that you, being rooted and grounded in love, may be able to comprehend with all the saints what is the breadth and length and height and depth, and to know the love of Christ which surpasses knowledge, that you may be filled up with all the fullness of God.

(Eph. 3:14–19)

Travail in prayer as Paul spoke of in Galatians 4:19. In a sense you are again pregnant, as Paul was, with their life,until Christ be formed in them. But only carry them in your heart (Phil. 1:7). You must not try to control, or you will drive them away from you, from the good values you have tried to instill in them during their formative years, and from the Lord.

13. As you cut your children free to take responsibility for their own lives, trust God and the deposit of love and nurture which has been built into them. Or, if you know those virtues to be seriously lacking in their foundations, make a decision to trust God's redemptive power.

If You Are a Single Parent:

Accept for yourself these words spoken to Israel:
" 'For your husband is your Maker, whose name is the LORD of hosts;
and your Redeemer is the Holy One of Israel, who is called the God of
all the earth. For the Lord has called you, like a wife forsaken and grieved in spirit, even like a wife of one's youth when she is
rejected,' says your God" (Isa. 54:5,6)

Remind yourself that your children are first of all a gift from God
(Ps. 127:3).

God promises to be a father to the fatherless (Ps. 68:5).

God takes responsibility for children who have been forsaken by both
father and mother (Ps. 27:10).

God promises to provide justice, food and clothing to the fatherless
(Deut. 10:18 and Deut. 14:29).

God is very present help in time of trouble (Ps. 46:1).

God will provide wisdom, knowledge, understanding and protection
for those who walk in His integrity (Prov. 2:6,7)

God will gird you with strength (Ps. 18:32).

God will answer your prayers (Matt. 21:22).

God shall supply all your needs (Phil. 4:19).

Your weeping will not last forever (Ps. 30:5).

"Be anxious for nothing, but in everything by prayer and supplication
with thanksgiving let your requests be made known to God. And the
peace of God, which surpasses all comprehension, shall guard your
hearts and your minds in Christ Jesus."   (Phil. 4:6,7).

**Are you walking around under a load of guilt because you
see your children in trouble and feel that you have failed
miserably in your task as a mother?**

Do you think that God did not know that you would make mistakes? He knew just exactly where, how, and how much you would fail, and He sent your children to you anyway. If you could have been a perfect mother, wouldn't your children have needed a Savior anyway? If you had been a perfect mother, do you believe your children would have made a perfect response to you? Not likely.

Everyone was created with free will; God did not want it any other way, because He does not want robots. He wants sons and daughters with whom to have fellowship. God is a perfect Father, yet all of His children except One need a Savior. There is not one who has not gone astray at some time. God is not therefore disqualified as a father. Jesus never sinned, but His disciples all failed Him, one of them to the extent of total betrayal. That does not disqualify Him to be the Lord of the universe. Neither are you disqualified by the failings of your children.

You and I have not been perfect mothers, but most of us have done the best we knew how. We ourselves have been maturing in the process, and though many of us are grandmothers, we are not all grown up yet. God loves us unconditionally and will not abandon us,

It is not our job to redeem the mistakes we have made with our children. That is the Lord's job. It is appropriate for us to repent and ask the Lord's and our children's forgiveness for all real and imagined guilts, and to *receive* forgiveness. Perhaps our children are not ready to forgive, but the Lord is. And it is His task to prepare their hearts.

It is our task to quit wallowing in self-punishing attitudes and actions, and to get on with daily living and loving to the utmost of our present capacity to allow the Lord to live and love in and through us.

A great deal of our children's healing comes as they relate, even remotely, to the process of healing in us. The more whole we become, the purer and more effective our prayers will be. Prayers of protection and blessing are appropriate even for our grown children.

You don't feel that you "deserve" to be forgiven? That's right. None of us deserve forgiveness. But since the Lord has already died for our sins on the cross, who do we think we are to keep on passing judgment on ourselves and say we don't "deserve" to receive what

He gave His life to make available to us? Or, you may know the Lord forgives you, but you just can't forgive yourself? If so, you've just installed yourself on a throne higher than God's. God will let us wallow in self-condemnation as long as we choose, but it is the antithesis of His nature and produces no good fruit whatsoever.

How can you have faith to believe that God is able to redeem your mistakes?

Isaiah 51:3 promises that God will comfort all our waste places, make our wildernesses like Eden, and our deserts like the garden of the Lord. But more powerful than promises are stories from real life. Of course the Bible is full of examples, and I have already shared some current testimonies. Let me share a few more from God's contemporary file.

Dan the Man

Dan was abandoned by his birth mother when he was less than five years old. To this day he has almost no memory of his natural parents. As a child, when people would ask him what happened to his father, sometimes he would say that his father had died, at other times that his father was serving a term in prison.

Dan was put in a foster home, and then another, and another, and...... In each home he would test his foster parents by his behavior, and when they had had enough, they would insist that he leave. By the time he was ten, he had gone through seven sets of foster parents and was placed with an eighth, a Christian family.

He soon started his practiced program of testing, and his foster mother told him, "Dan, we know what you are doing, and we want you to know that we are not going to get rid of you for any reason — so you may as well just settle down and decide to get along with us." He did, and when he was eleven, his new family adopted him. His adoptive mother was affectionate, and he thrived on hugs.

One outstanding and aggravating problem prevailed. Toys had been provided for Dan in most of the homes where he had stayed, but nothing was his to keep. Each time he was assigned to new foster parents, even birthday presents stayed behind! Over the years he had developed an attitude that anything that wasn't nailed down was his to take and use for as long as he could manage to keep it.

In his new family, toys, tools, and money disappeared regularly, and when he was confronted with undeniable evidence, it became apparent he had no conscience concerning the thefts. He had no concept of personal property. Again and again family members would say to him, "Dan, what do we call it when someone takes something that belongs to another without asking their permission, and then fails to return it?"

Dan would mouth the answer, "stealing," and listen to the warning not to do it again, but would soon demonstrate that the principle had not yet become a part of him. We knew the family and understood that a part of his compulsion to steal had to do with deep feelings that his life had been stolen from him. He therefore was living out the opposite of the Golden Rule, doing to others what had been done to him.

Dan attended church services regularly with his new family. One morning a woman visitor in the congregation sat next to him. After a while Dan left the service to check on his little brother. The woman followed him into the hall. She called him by name. He turned around, puzzled that she seemed to know him. Yet, there was something familiar about her.

She handed him a note, "Dan, I'm your real mother. I left you a long time ago because I couldn't take care of you. Since then I've become a Christian, and God directed me to come to this church this morning. He wants me to ask your forgiveness for the way I hurt you. Will you forgive me?" Dan was stunned, but he voiced his forgiveness. The woman then ran out of the church, weeping.

Dan was deeply touched by the incident and shared it with his adoptive parents and the pastor. The pastor had noticed the woman's distress and had been disappointed that he was unable to talk with her after the service. He saw her in the community some time later and approached her, asking her about the incident. She denied then that she had ever had a son.

But Dan's momentary meeting with her that Sunday morning had a lasting effect on him. God had given him a precious gift — the opportunity to objectify what had only lived in his fantasies, and a chance to express forgiveness. He no longer had a hidden longing to search after the woman who claimed to be his mother. Something in him came to rest because he knew that God had taken the initiative to do something very special for him. Dan knew his adoptive father had also been wounded when *his* natural mother gave *him* away, and he commented, "I sure wish something like that could happen for Dad!"

Dan struggled through his high school years, finding it difficult to be consistent in his studies. Finishing projects was never easy for him. He spent a great deal more time taking his motorcycle apart than he did riding it. Despite unconditional love and acceptance from his entire extended adoptive family, he had problems with self-esteem. It showed in his dress. He would invariably by-pass good tee-shirts and jeans to wear something torn, and stained with grease.

Whatever security Dan had felt at home was shattered when his adoptive father fell into gross sin, and the family was broken by divorce. He maintained relationships with the rest of his family, but he dropped out of school, wandered around jobless for a while, mooching off his friends, and finally settled in with a group of ne'er-do-wells. He found a job and worked hard at it but he and his roommates partied a lot.

After a while he began to resent being the one who had to pay the rent while his so-called friends mooched off him and partied. "This is nothin' but a dead end," he decided. With that, he abandoned his partying friends, the booze, and the drugs, took tests for a high school equivalency diploma, and searched out and obtained financial aid so that he could get some vocational training. He enrolled in the local college, and started attending church again.

Two years later he graduated at the top of his class and has been working ever since as a skilled marine mechanic as well as serving in the army reserve. Restored self-esteem shows both in his dress and manly demeanor. And he has been reconciled to his adoptive father who has also received a good measure of the Lord's merciful redemptive power.

We know Dan had one mother travailing for him in prayer. I suspect he had two.

From Latrines to Riches

When we first met Jodie, she was one of those young women about whom you find yourself thinking. "She could really be beautiful if she would lose about fifty pounds. Our hearts broke for her as she poured out her feelings of low self-esteem and loneliness, the hopelessness she had concerning her future, the despair she felt concerning any possibility of experiencing significant change.

Jodie's parents had divorced, and she was living with her extremely bitter and possessive mother who relentlessly poured out a vitriolic stream of self-pity and resentment against her former husband. Jodie had no boyfriend, no social life, and little opportunity to develop friendships. Though she had great undeveloped musical ability, she worked steadily as a janitor in a large public building where she specialized in cleaning toilets.

After counseling with Jodie for several weeks we began to talk with her about her future. We suggested that she go back to school to develop her musical talent or whatever else her heart yearned for. We talked with her about scholarships and other financial aids. But we kept running up against a wall of futility in her.

It became apparent that she had accepted an oft-repeated lie that she couldn't dare to leave her hurting mother — that somehow her mother's welfare depended on her remaining at home. She felt compelled to sacrifice her life to be her mother's rock and emotional refuge. We, and her father, had to persist patiently in prayer and conversation with her before she was able to recognize that she had been emotionally manipulated until she had finally become a prisoner of delusion.

Despite her mother's loud protests, she was finally able to cut free. She enrolled in a university far from her home, pursued her musical training, graduated with honors, lost more than fifty pounds, and married a fine Christian man.

Without her, Jodie's mother did not die — not even to her own self-centered attitudes — and certainly not to her anger toward us as the ones who persuaded her daughter to break free. But God isn't finished with her yet.

The importance of this story is to say that even though a misguided mother may travail with sinful motivations for all the wrong purposes, God is still able to rescue His children, set them on a healthy track, and bring them into the glory He has prepared for them.

Hope for Today and Tomorrow

Today it certainly appears that dysfunctional families are becoming the norm, and the lives of few children are being built on foundations without serious fractures. At the same time, the Lord is pouring His Holy Spirit upon ALL mankind (Joel 2:28), not just Christians. This means that people everywhere are being quickened to search hungrily not only for intellectual answers to problems, but for spiritual realities to comfort their hearts and fill their emptiness. Many are receiving Jesus as Lord and Savior, so that the Holy Spirit falls rightly into their hearts.

But some who have become disillusioned with the Christian church, and many who are unloved, untaught and undisciplined, are extremely vulnerable and, without discernment, are searching in new age philosophies and occultism. When they feed on Satan's counterfeits which cannot satisfy, they tend to crave more and more because they have swallowed the lying promise of belonging and fulfillment and power. Satan seems to be able to come up with enough deceptive spiritual titillations to keep them on the hook.

At the same time thousands of jean-clad young people are flocking to churches which present the gospel through a contemporary style of music in worship which communicates a clear Jesus-now-His-

Presence-with-me-and-His-Spirit-living-in-me message of hope. They are unwilling to settle with going through the motions of being Christian, or playing games. They want to be accepted just as they are into a *family* which offers unconditional nurturing love. They long to experience the power of a living God to change lives.

The Church is called to be an organism of family groups in which individual members lay down their lives for one another, that each person may receive the nurturing foundation which their natural family was unequipped to provide. This is what St. Paul was praying for in Ephesians 3:

> So that Christ may dwell in your hearts through faith; and that you, **being rooted and grounded in love,** may be able to comprehend with all the saints what is the breadth and length and height and depth, and to know the love of Christ which surpasses knowledge, that you may be filled up to all the fullness of God.   (Eph. 3:17-19)

With that quality of foundational preparation, the Church is called to go into all the world and preach the gospel.

In this day we are not only beginning to see the lame healed and sight restored to the blind. We are seeing homosexuals delivered from confusion and restored to God's original wholesome intent.

Counselors used to minister largely to those who were basically fairly sound, but needed forgiveness and some readjustment so they could continue to grow up emotionally and spiritually. Now they are often ministering to those who have been ritualistically abused, those who are coming out of cults, and many who have been so damaged as children that they have developed multiple personalities and other complex disorders.

By the grace, the revelation, and the power of God many of these wounded ones are being healed. But there is often such a depth of hurt and anxiety in them that even after receiving the Lord they need a great deal of prayer to prepare their hearts to accept and walk in their healing.

Mothers — Travail for Your Children!

Out of the depths I have cried to Thee, O LORD. Lord, hear my voice! Let Thine ears be attentive to the voice of my supplications.

If Thou, LORD, shouldst mark iniquities, O Lord, who could stand?

But there is forgiveness with Thee, that Thou mayest be feared.

I Wait for the Lord, my soul does wait and in His word do I hope. . . . O Israel, hope in the LORD; for with the LORD there is lovingkindness, and with Him there is abundant redemption." (Ps. 30:1-7)

"And we know that God causes all things to work together for good to those who love God, to those who are called according to *His* purpose." (Rom. 8:28)

Christians — Travail for the Children of This Generation!
BE the Church!

I am aware that the words "Zion" and "Jerusalem" in the Bible are believed by many to refer to the Jewish nation. Others insist that in some instances these names refer to the Church. Others like myself believe that both views are correct in the light of Romans 10:11 and 12:

> For the Scripture says, "WHOEVER BELIEVES IN HIM WILL NOT BE DISAPPOINTED." For there is no distinction between Jew and Greek; for the same *Lord* is Lord of all, abounding in riches for all who call upon Him; for "WHOEVER WILL CALL UPON THE NAME OF THE LORD WILL BE SAVED."

I invite you to consider the following Scripture as a *rhema* word to you as a part of the Body of Christ.

> As soon as Zion travailed, she also brought forth her sons. "Shall I bring to the point of birth, and not give delivery?" says the LORD. "Or shall I who gives delivery shut the womb?" says your God.

> "Be joyful for Jerusalem and rejoice for her, all you who love her; be exceedingly glad for her, all you who mourn over her, that you may be satisfied with her comforting breasts, that you may suck and be delighted with her bountiful bosom." For thus says the LORD, "Behold, I extend peace to her like a river, and the glory of the nations like

an overflowing stream; and you shall be nursed, you shall be carried on the hip and fondled on the knees. As one whom his mother comforts, so I will comfort you, and you shall be comforted in Jerusalem."

Then you shall see this, and your heart shall be glad, and your bones shall flourish like the new grass; and the hand of the LORD shall be made known to His servants, but He shall be indignant toward His enemies.
(Isa. 66:8b-14)

The Body of Christ, the Church, is called to be a nurturing body for broken families, and a healing body for the nations. Christians must learn to carry others in their hearts and to travail in prayer for the children as Paul did, "My children, with whom I am again in labor until Christ be formed in you" (Gal. 4:19). Those children will then have opportunity to "grow up in all aspects into him, who is the head, even Christ" (Eph. 4:15b), and bring healing to many more.

Women are naturally equipped with faith and stamina for labor in childbirth. "Whenever a woman is in travail she has sorrow, because her hour has come, but when she gives birth to the child, she remembers the anguish no more, for joy that a child has been born into the world" (John 16:21). In ministry she has only to transfer what she knows in the natural to the task which both men and women are called to do in the spiritual.

God has created women with a special gift of tenderness which nurtures. In First Thessalonians 2:6,7 Paul speaks of his ministry, along with Sylvanus and Timothy having been successful largely because of the way they had chosen to emulate that gift rather than assert their authority. "But we proved to be gentle among you, as a nursing mother tenderly cares for her own children."

It is important that we remember that though there is no male or female in Christ (Gal. 3:27,28), that is, we are all one in Him, there are many distinctly female attributes which we should cherish. Each of us will grow into the freedom to be and express all that we are when we can say, "Thank you, God, for making me me." And when we enter into a relationship with Him who is our primary source of love, hope, strength, affirmation and peace.

Afterword

As I conclude this book I am well aware that I have only begun to speak to the many issues which deeply impact the hearts of women. What about aging? The myths we believe about beauty? The way we feel about our bodies? Sexual confusions and dysfunctions? The problems we encounter in the marketplace? And many others. A second book is birthing in my mind. You can help me by expressing your concerns and needs and by sharing your testimonies.

Write to me in care of:
Elijah House, Inc.
S. 1000 Richards Rd.
Post Falls, Idaho, 83854

Bibliography

The Holy Bible, New American Standard Version, unless otherwise indicated.

Levine, Rachel, "The Biblical Woman," *YAVO Digest,* Vol. 3, No. 6.

Smalley, Gary and Trent, John, "Why Can't My Spouse Understand What I Say?," *Focus on the Family,* Nov., 1988.

Dobson, Dr. James, "The Second Great Civil War," *Focus on the Family,* Nov., 1990.

Wight, Fred H., *Manners and Customs of Bible Lands,* Moody Press, 1989.

ELIJAH HOUSE MINISTRY CATALOG

A catalog is available from Elijah House that lists products and resources in the following categories:

I. **COUNSELOR RESOURCES** — *Unique tools of reference for any counseling office.* Audio tapes: Theology of Healing; The Healing Process; Healing Early Experiences; Burnout; Responses and Behaviors; Healing Spiritual Wounds; Healing Sexual Abuse; Chemical Dependency.

II. **MINISTRY TRAINING TOOLS** — *Practical teaching for pastors and church leaders.* Audio tapes and manuals: Divine Doctoring of Small Groups; Prayer Ministry Teams; New Testament Church; Prayer Ministry Teams.

III. **ADULT EDUCATION** — *Terrific curriculum for adult study.* Audio tapes: Life in Christ; Healing the Wounded Spirit; Renewal of the Mind; Twelve Functions of the Prophetic Office; Nurturing the Prophetic; What God Is Saying to the Church.

IV. **PERSONAL STUDY LIBRARY** — *Anyone can benefit from these teachings about marriage, children, and understanding ourselves.* Audio and video tapes: Before You Say 'I Do'; Married Forever; For Men Only; Functions of a Father's Love; Ministering to Youth and Children; Parental Love; Keeping Your Healing; Living a Full Live!' Comfortably Corporate; Garlands for Ashes; How Could It Happen?; Life's Common Sexual Experiences; Homosexuality.

V. **BOOKS** — *Ground-breaking books about inner healing and issues facing the Church today.* The Transformation of the Inner Man, Restoring the Christian Family; Healing the Wounded Spirit; The Elijah Task; Why Some Christians Commit Adultery; Healing Victims of Sexual Abuse; The Renewal of the Mind; Wounded Warriors; Healing Womens' Emotions.

Write to:
Elijah House
1000 S. Richards Road
Post Falls, ID 83854

BEST SELLER!
OVER 200,000 SOLD

We all desire wholeness. We see our need for inner healing. All too often, however, we find it is an elusive goal.

The individual reader and the counselor alike will thrill at the insights — and personal revelations — imparted by this life-transforming book!

A HANDBOOK FOR FAMILIES

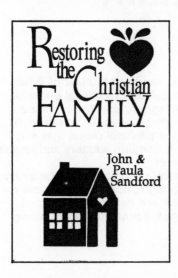

"And He shall turn the heart of the fathers to the children, and the heart of the children to their fathers" (Mal. 4:6). God is restoring families to His original purpose — to be the foundation of society, the seedbed for Christian values. Those who have discovered this treasure chest of teaching report that it has transformed their families. Fresh insights from the Sandfords' teaching and counseling ministry will enable your family to grow and develop according to God's plan.

AVAILABLE AT CHRISTIAN BOOKSTORES EVERYWHERE.

INNER HEALING CLASSIC

This sequel continues in the footsteps of **The Transformation of the Inner Man** by providing new insight and healing salve to such problems as rejection, child abuse, occult involvement and generational sin and depression.

Healing the Wounded Spirit is for everyone who suffers from hidden hurts — past or present. Through this book, God can help you to discern a wounded spirit in yourself and others and, best of all, He will show you how to receive His healing power in your life.

WHY ADULTERY?

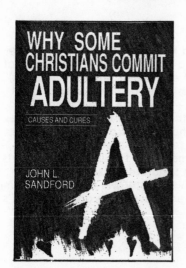

John L. Sandford founder of Elijah House, and author of several books on inner healing, provides answers for all who are concerned about this issue. He explores the personal causes that may lead a Christian into adultery and reveals biblical cures.

The book's main purpose, the author states, "is to provide informed bases for compassion and healing, and keys of knowledge for protection from falling."

AVAILABLE AT CHRISTIAN BOOKSTORES EVERYWHERE.

PROPHETIC INSIGHT

In the **Elijah Task,** John and Paula Sandford give a clear message, a balanced and practical in-depth study of the office of a prophet in the church and world today, the power and ways of inter-cession, and prophetic listening to God.

TRANSFORMED BY THE RENEWING OF YOUR MIND!

THE RENEWAL OF THE MIND glows with fresh insights and anointing. Its revolutionary approach will still the battleground where carnal thoughts and feelings rage. There is a solution — a pro-cess of spiritual transformation by the renewing of your mind. As you read, new peace and life will fill your innermost being.

AVAILABLE AT CHRISTIAN BOOKSTORES EVERYWHERE.

HEALING FOR THE WOUNDS OF STRESS

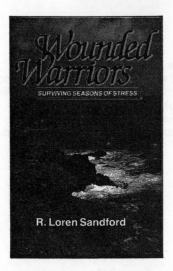

The author of *Wounded Warriors*, Pastor R. Loren Sandford, knows what it's like to be in a stressed out and wounded condition, as he came near to a total breakdown while ministering to others.

His book provides believers with an honest look at stress — its symptoms, causes and effects — and it shows how to deal with this all-too-common problem in effective, lasting ways. For the person who lives with or counsels a wounded warrior, this book imparts empathy and wisdom. For the wounded warrior himself, this book imparts hope, peace and healing.

RESTORATION FOR THE ABUSED

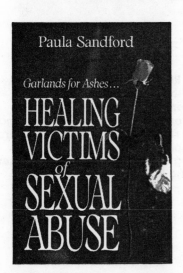

With profound empathy and clear understanding, Paula Sandford ministers healing to all who have been victimized by sexual abuse — the abused child, parents, relatives and friends, as well as the abuser. She has dealt with this problem through many years of counseling and teaching, and this book shows how the victims of sexual abuse can find new life and freedom.

AVAILABLE AT CHRISTIAN BOOKSTORES EVERYWHERE.

BOOK ORDER FORM

To order additional books by John and Paula Sandford or Loren Sandford direct from the publisher, please use this order form. Also note that your local bookstore can order titles for you.

Book Title	Price	Quantity	Amount
Healing Womens' Emotions	$ 9.95	_____	$ _____
Why Some Christians Commit Adultery	$ 9.95	_____	$ _____
Healing Victims of Sexual Abuse	$ 8.95	_____	$ _____
The Transformation of the Inner Man	$10.95	_____	$ _____
Healing the Wounded Spirit	$11.95	_____	$ _____
Restoring the Christian Family	$10.95	_____	$ _____
The Elijah Task	$ 9.95	_____	$ _____
Wounded Warriors (by L. Sandford)	$ 7.95	_____	$ _____
Total Book Amount			$ _____
Shipping & Handling — Add $2.00 for the **first** book, **plus** $0.50 for **each** additional book			$ _____
TOTAL ORDER AMOUNT — Enclose check or money order (No cash or C.O.D.'s)			$ _____

Make check or money order payable to: **VICTORY HOUSE, INC.**
Mail order to: **VICTORY HOUSE, INC.**
        P.O. Box 700238
        Tulsa, OK 74170

Please print your name and address **clearly:**

Name _____

Address _____

City _____

State or Province _____

Zip or Postal Code _____

Telephone Number (_____) _____

Foreign orders must be submitted in U.S. dollars. Foreign orders are shipped by uninsured surface mail. We ship all orders within 48 hours of receipt of order.

MasterCard or VISA — For orders totaling **over $20.00** you may use your MasterCard or VISA by completing the following information or for **faster service** call toll-free **1-800-262-2631.**

Card Name_____

Card Number _____

Expiration Date _____

Signature_____
                    (authorized signature)